Two and Two Together

A comedy

Derek Benfield

Samuel French — London
New York - Toronto - Hollywood

© 1999 BY DEREK BENFIELD

Rights of Performance by Amateurs are controlled by Samuel French Ltd, 52 Fitzroy Street, London W1P 6JR, and they, or their authorized agents, issue licences to amateurs on payment of a fee. **It is an infringement of the Copyright to give any performance or public reading of the play before the fee has been paid and the licence issued.**

The Royalty Fee indicated below is subject to contract and subject to variation at the sole discretion of Samuel French Ltd.

Basic fee for each and every
    performance by amateurs   Code M
    in the British Isles

The Professional Rights in this play are controlled by Lemon Unna and Durbridge Ltd, 24 Pottery Lane, Holland Park, London W11 4LZ

The publication of this play does not imply that it is necessarily available for performance by amateurs or professionals, either in the British Isles or Overseas. Amateurs and professionals considering a production are strongly advised in their own interests to apply to the appropriate agents for consent before starting rehearsals or booking a theatre or hall.

ISBN 0 573 01947 9

Please see page iv for further copyright information

TWO AND TWO TOGETHER

CHARACTERS
(in order of appearance)

Frank, a young man pursued by Rachel

Rachel, Victor's wife, in pursuit of Frank

Victor, a businessman, in pursuit of Georgina

Georgina, Henry's wife, pursued by Victor

Procter, a man—with a dog—who watches

Henry, an actor, unaware of possible infidelity

Mrs Capstick, a cleaning lady who listens

The events take place in two houses in the same street in the suburbs of a big city, one belonging to Georgina and Henry, the other to Rachel and Victor

ACT I   A Thursday evening in summer
ACT II   The next morning, ten o'clock

Time: the present

Two and Two Together

The play was first produced at the Contra-Kreis Theatre in Bonn, Germany, on November 6th, 1997, with the following cast:

Frank	Christophorus Heufken
Rachel	Rotraut Reiger
Victor	Holger Petsold
Georgina	Birgit Vogel
Procter	Jochen Stern
Henry	Rainer Delventhal
Mrs Capstick	Samy Orfgen

The play was directed by **Horst Johanning**
Setting by **Pit Fischer**

Other plays by Derek Benfield
published by Samuel French Ltd:

Anyone for Breakfast?
Bedside Manners
Beyond a Joke
A Bird in the Hand
Caught on the Hop
Don't Lose the Place!
Fish Out of Water
A Fly in the Ointment
Flying Feathers
In for the Kill
Look Who's Talking
Murder for the Asking
Off the Hook!
Panic Stations
Post Horn Gallop
Running Riot
A Toe in the Water
Touch and Go
Up and Running
Wild Goose Chase

ACT I

The reception rooms of two houses, one belonging to Georgina and Henry, the other to Rachel and Victor. The houses are a little distance apart in the same street in the suburbs of a big city. The stage is in two halves: Georgina's and Henry's house is R, Rachel's and Victor's L. They are contrasting in design and furnishing. It is a Thursday evening in summer and the sun is shining

The front doors of both houses are UC. In Georgina's and Henry's there is a door to the kitchen UR and an archway DR which leads to the staircase and bedrooms. In Rachel's and Victor's the kitchen door is DL and a door leading to the hall and bedrooms is UL with a window seat between it and the front door. Each house has a sofa of differing style which adjoins the one in the other house, each with a table above it. Georgina and Henry have a low armchair DR with a small coffee table beside it, a box seat below the kitchen door and a chest of drawers against the centre wall. There is a recessed shelf and cupboard unit R of the front door, where the drinks and stereo are kept, and L of the front door is an umbrella stand. Rachel and Victor have a drinks cupboard against the C wall, a crescent table above the kitchen door with a wastepaper basket below it, and a coffee table below the sofa. (See ground plan on page 84)

The Lights come up on Georgina's and Henry's house. Someone is outside knocking on the front door

Frank, a shy man in his thirties, looks in from the kitchen. He is wearing a lady's apron and is a bit agitated. He calls to the person outside

Frank Come in!

Frank goes back into the kitchen

The knocking starts again

Frank reappears, a little more agitated

Come in! Come in!

Frank goes again

More loud knocking

Frank looks in and bellows, loudly

It's open! Push it, push it, push it!

Frank disappears back into the kitchen

The front door opens and Rachel falls in, breathlessly. She is an attractive woman in her late forties, wearing a track-suit, trainers and a peaked yachting cap back-to-front. She carries a sports bag which she casts aside and closes the front door

Frank comes in, no longer wearing the apron

Rachel looks at him, apprehensively

Rachel You're not in a bad mood, are you?
Frank No… (*More firmly*) No. (*But he is*)
Rachel Yes, you are. I can tell. You shouted three times.
Frank Well, the door was open. You didn't have to knock.
Rachel I didn't think you'd have left it open. (*She collapses on to the sofa, exhausted*)
Frank I was in the kitchen.
Rachel What were you doing in there?
Frank (*self-consciously*) Cooking.
Rachel (*smiling in disbelief*) Cooking?
Frank I *can* cook!
Rachel Yes. When you're at home. But you haven't cooked *here* before.
Frank Some little bits to go with the aperitif.
Rachel Is that what we're having? Little bits and an aperitif?
Frank You know what I mean!
Rachel I certainly do. An aperitif is something you have *first*.
Frank Yes.
Rachel Before something else. (*She smiles, encouragingly*)
Frank Yes…
Rachel Little bits and an aperitif, and then something else? (*She chuckles, enjoying his embarrassment*)
Frank (*suddenly*) Oh, my God.
Rachel What's the matter?
Frank My little bits'll be burning!

Frank runs out into the kitchen

Brisk music plays as Rachel stands up and removes her track-suit top, revealing the top part of a dress. She then removes the trousers and we see that the dress has been tucked up around her waist. She deftly releases it. It hangs immaculately! The music stops

Frank returns with a plate of cocktail savouries—sausages, mini vol-au-vents, etc. He is staring at the plate as he approaches and does not yet see her transformation

Rachel Have your "bits" survived?
Frank I'm not sure. (*He looks up and sees her dress. He jumps with surprise and drops the plate of savouries*) Ah!! (*He kneels down and hastily starts to gather them up*) You gave me such a shock. Why are you dressed up like that?
Rachel Don't you like it? (*She pirouettes to show it off*)
Frank (*grinning*) Trainers don't help much.

Rachel dashes away to her sports bag, takes off her trainers and replaces them with a pair of more suitable, high-heeled shoes. She returns to him, elegantly

Rachel Better now?
Frank (*gazing in admiration*) Yes—great…
Rachel That's all right, then. (*She sits down again*) Well? Aren't you going to give me one?
Frank Sorry?
Rachel One of your "bits"!
Frank Oh. Yes. Right. (*He holds out the plate of savouries*)

Rachel takes a cocktail sausage and starts to eat it

All right?
Rachel H'm. Delicious. I never realized that carpet tasted so good.
Frank I'll get the drinks.
Rachel Great!
Frank (*impressively*) We're having … champagne.
Rachel Really? Why?
Frank Well, it is a special occasion.
Rachel Is it?
Frank We've been doing this now for three weeks.
Rachel I didn't think we'd done *anything* yet…

Frank Meeting here and getting to know each other!
Rachel Oh—that. Yes…
Frank So I got champagne. I thought it would be romantic.
Rachel Sorry?
Frank (*a little put out*) Don't you know what it means?
Rachel Of course I know what it means. But we could have been romantic and got to know each other down at the rowing club. We didn't need all this subterfuge.
Frank I thought it was something to celebrate…
Rachel (*smiling, warmly*) Yes, Frank—of course it is.
Frank (*cheering up*) Right! You wait here.

Frank runs out to the kitchen and returns with an ice bucket and two champagne glasses

He puts them down on the table behind the sofa and (with great effect) produces a very small bottle of champagne from inside the ice bucket. Rachel tries to look suitably impressed. Frank opens the mini-bottle and pours two glasses. He brings one to Rachel, and then goes to sit down in the armchair a little distance away from her

Happy anniversary!
Rachel Sorry?
Frank Three weeks…
Rachel Oh, yes. Cheers!

They raise their glasses and drink. Frank sighs, contentedly

Frank It's very good of your friend to lend you her house occasionally.
Rachel Well, Georgina and I were at school together. We bonded during the biology class, so now she'll do anything for me.
Frank So what's *she* doing tonight?
Rachel Going to the pictures, I think. Does it matter? She's not here and we *are*, that's all that matters. (*She smiles at him, encouragingly*)
Frank What about her husband? *He*'s not likely to turn up, is he?
Rachel I told you—he's an actor! He works in the theatre every evening. He's never back till late.
Frank (*relaxing*) That's all right, then. (*He sips his champagne*)
Rachel Frank…
Frank H'm?
Rachel Why don't you come and sit over here?
Frank (*blankly*) Sorry?
Rachel After three weeks surely you can sit next to me on the sofa.

Frank Oh. Yes. Right. (*He gets up and goes to sit beside her*)
Rachel That's better. Now I've got you in my sights.

Frank gets up again. Rachel restrains him

  Where are you going *now*?
Frank Er—to close the front door.
Rachel I closed it.
Frank Oh. Right. (*He sits down again, then starts to get up once more*)

Again she restrains him

Rachel Frank!—
Frank You might not have locked it.
Rachel (*a little impatient*) Yes, I did—come and sit down!

He sits down next to her again

A pause

He picks up the plate of "bits"

Frank Would you like another sausage?

Rachel laughs, and abandons the unequal contest

Rachel No, thanks. I think I'll try one of these fishy things. (*She takes a vol-au-vent and enjoys it*)

Frank helps himself to a sausage and eats it, thoughtfully

Frank Does he *really* think you're rowing?
Rachel (*eating*) Sorry?
Frank Victor. Your husband! Does he really think you're rowing?
Rachel Well, he doesn't think I'm eating sausages.
Frank Won't he think it rather odd?
Rachel Why should he?
Frank Well … going rowing … and arriving home with a dress on underneath your track-suit.
Rachel Don't be silly. I won't be going home in it. Will I?
Frank Won't you?
Rachel Presumably I shall have taken it off before then. Won't I?
Frank Will you?

Rachel I hope so! Is there any more in that bottle?

Frank hastily gets the tiny bottle and tries to squeeze out the last drop—without success. He looks at the empty bottle, dispiritedly. Rachel grins at him, gets up and starts to go with her empty glass

Come on!
Frank Where are we going?
Rachel Let's see if we can find something bigger in the kitchen!

Rachel marches out into the kitchen

Frank throws the empty bottle into the ice bucket, picks it up and follows her as——

The Lights fade to Black-out

The Lights come up on Rachel's and Victor's house. The doorbell is ringing

Victor, a good-looking businessman in his fifties, comes in from the kitchen, hastily picking up his jacket and putting it on before opening the front door

Georgina is there, holding a small evening bag. She is a very pretty, rather nervous lady about the same age as Rachel

Victor (*warmly*) Georgina! (*He holds out his arms, welcomingly*)

She darts in past him, ignoring his welcoming arms. Victor closes the door and looks at her, apprehensively

You're not in a bad mood, are you?
Georgina No… (*More firmly*) No! (*But she is*)
Victor Yes, you are. I can tell. You rang the bell three times.
Georgina Well, why didn't you leave the door open? I felt so self-conscious standing out there in broad daylight. *Anyone* could have seen me.
Victor Nothing wrong with that. You weren't trying to break in.
Georgina Suppose someone *had* seen me and asked what I was doing here? I couldn't tell the truth, could I?
Victor You could have made something up. That's what people do in situations like this. Invent.
Georgina I can't invent! I'm not used to situations like this.
Victor (*trying to reassure her*) You just need a bit of practice.

Georgina Oh, I'm really fed up…
Victor Yes. I can see you are.

Georgina sinks on to the sofa, despondently

Georgina Do you think all this is a good idea?
Victor We won't know till we've tried it.
Georgina I mean me coming *here*—to your house! (*She loses heart even more*) It's no good. I'd better go. (*She gets up and starts to go*)

Victor intercepts her, amused by her lack of sophistication

Victor Then whoever may have seen you coming *in* will see you going *out*.
Georgina That's all right. I've only been here a *minute*. Nothing much can happen in a minute. Can it? (*Suddenly inspired*) I could have been delivering a leaflet!

He smiles at her, delightedly

Victor You see? You're learning already!
Georgina (*pleased with her progress*) Good. That's what I'll say then. (*She starts to go*)

Victor catches her

Victor No.
Georgina No?
Victor (*as to a child*) You'd have put a leaflet through the letter-box.
Georgina Oh … yes. (*Hopefully*) A parcel?
Victor (*laughing*) No, no! Anyone who saw you coming in would know you didn't have a parcel with you.
Georgina (*desperately*) What shall I do, then?
Victor Stay and have a drink.
Georgina You think I should?
Victor That *was* the idea. (*He chuckles and heads for the drinks*) Gin-and-tonic?
Georgina That would be nice.
Victor Ice and lemon?
Georgina Yes, please. (*She sits on the sofa*)

Victor prepares the drinks. Georgina watches him, and notices something

You're all dressed up!

Victor Yes. I've been to work. I always dress up when I go to work. It's
    Saturdays and Sundays when I don't dress up. (*Helpfully*) I'll take my
    trousers off if you like.
Georgina (*giggling*) I think we'd better have a drink first!
Victor Well, don't say I didn't offer. (*He returns with their drinks and sits
    beside her*) Cheers!
Georgina Cheers!

They drink

Victor It was certainly our lucky day, wasn't it?
Georgina Sorry?
Victor Three weeks ago!
Georgina (*lost for a moment*) Oh. What happened then?
Victor Rachel took up rowing!
Georgina Is *that* when she started? Three weeks ago?
Victor Yes.
Georgina I ... I'd forgotten.
Victor So why didn't *we* take up *this* three weeks ago?
Georgina I suppose we hadn't thought of it then.
Victor Yes, we had!
Georgina Had we?
Victor Well, *I* had.
Georgina So had I.
Victor We just didn't get around to it.
Georgina No, I suppose not. (*Suddenly a little put out*) So we're three weeks
    behind.
Victor Sorry?
Georgina Well, *she*'s been doing it for three weeks, and this is only our first
    attempt.

Victor thinks about this

Victor Yes. But Rachel's only *rowing*…
Georgina (*quickly*) Ah—yes! Yes, I know that! That's what she's doing all
    right—rowing!
Victor Well ... we're *not* rowing, are we? That's the difference.
Georgina We're still three weeks behind…
Victor Then we'd better catch up, hadn't we? (*He puts down his glass, takes
    hers and puts it down also. He moves closer to her, his face near to hers,
    gazing into her eyes*)

*They remain like that, motionless, for a moment. Then Georgina loses
confidence*

Georgina I don't think I'm in the mood.

Victor But we've only got two hours! How long does it take to get in the mood?

Georgina Now you're cross.

Victor I'm not cross. It was you who said we were three weeks behind.

Georgina Perhaps I'll be better when I've finished my gin. (*She rescues her glass and drinks, gratefully*)

Victor smiles, amused by her delightful innocence, and sips his own gin. He chuckles at something that has occurred to him

What are you laughing at?

Victor I was just thinking—if Rachel came back early from rowing and found us here like this she'd never believe that nothing had been going on!

Georgina (*confidently*) She *won't* come back early.

Victor You can't be sure.

Georgina (*smiling secretly*) Yes, I can…!

Victor How?

Georgina Well … people who row don't give up in the middle and come home.

Victor They would if they were sinking. If she's only been doing it for three weeks she may not have got into the swing of it yet. She might get tired and give up halfway through.

Georgina (*giggling at the thought*) Oh, I think she's better at it than that…!

Victor I jolly well hope so.

Georgina Don't worry. She won't come back early.

Victor Good. I'll take my clothes off then. (*He gets up and takes off his jacket*)

Georgina No!

Victor What?

Georgina Didn't you say something about food?

Victor Did I? When was that?

Georgina On the telephone. You said we'd probably have something to eat first.

Victor Did *I* say that?

Georgina Yes.

Victor (*glancing at his watch*) Well, we don't have a lot of time, do we?

Georgina (*disappointed*) No time for food?

Victor I don't think we've anything in.

Georgina Nothing in the deep freeze?

Victor Afraid not.

Georgina I thought you'd done this sort of thing before.

Victor (*sheepishly*) No… Anyway, *I'm* providing the accommodation. I don't expect to do the catering as well.

Georgina You should have asked me to pick up some sandwiches on the way!

Victor (*giving in, happily*) All right, come on then! (*He takes her hand and leads her towards the kitchen*) Perhaps we can find you a bar of chocolate.

Georgina and Victor go into the kitchen as the Lights fade to Black-out

The Lights come up on Georgina's and Henry's house. Someone is outside, knocking on the door

Rachel comes out of the kitchen and goes to the door, uncertainly

Rachel Who is it?

Procter (*off*) Neighbourhood Watch! Open up!

Rachel Oh, my God…! (*She opens the front door*)

Procter is there, his unseen dog pulling at his leash and barking. He is a large man in his sixties

Rachel stares at him, impatiently

    What do you want?

Procter I'm here to help.

Rachel I don't *need* any help!

Procter Is everything all right?

Rachel No, it isn't…!

Procter Just as I thought. I'd better come in.

The dog outside barks again

Rachel Leave that outside! I can't have dogs in here!

Procter Oh. Right. (*To his dog*) Sit! Sit… Good boy. Now stay. Stay… (*He nods, approvingly, to the dog, casts the leash to the ground and steps inside*)

Rachel closes the door and follows him into the room

Rachel What are you doing here?

Procter I was passing.

Rachel Then you should have gone *on* passing.

Procter My name is Procter.

Rachel Even so.

Procter I'm an enthusiastic member of Neighbourhood Watch. (*He moves further into the room, looking about, eagerly*)

Rachel (*following him, nervously*) Well, there's nothing to watch *here*!

Procter (*consulting his notebook*) You're on my list as being unoccupied tonight.

Rachel I think there's been a mistake——

Procter Exactly! You're occupied when you should be *un*occupied. I was walking my dog when we spotted movement.

Rachel Movement? Where?

Procter In here! So we thought we'd better investigate. (*He moves below the sofa, looking about*) Is there a burglar on the premises?

Rachel No!

Procter (*surprised*) *Not* a burglar?

Rachel Definitely not! I'm here on my own.

Procter But we heard voices.

Rachel We were listening to the radio. (*Hastily correcting herself*) I was listening to the radio!

Procter misinterprets her anxiety and looks about, furtively, then leans closer to her and whispers

Procter Don't be frightened. If there's anyone hiding, just point me in the right direction. I'm quite at home with such emergencies. I used to be in the SAS.

Rachel (*whispering also*) But there's nobody here!

Procter (*loudly, for the sake of the unseen burglar*) Are you quite sure there's nobody here?

Rachel (*loudly also*) Of course I'm sure!

Procter (*whispering again*) Good! You're doing well. You have lulled the villain into a false sense of security. Now—call him! And when he appears I'll pounce!

Rachel But there *is* no villain!

Procter (*disappointed*) No villain?

Rachel No.

Procter What a pity. I haven't pounced for weeks.

Rachel (*quietly*) Neither have I...!

Procter I apologise for disturbing you, but we have to be sure. Quite often there are hidden intruders. So you're not in any danger of rape?

Rachel (*ruefully*) I shouldn't think so...!

Procter suddenly realizes something and looks at her more closely

Procter Wait a minute! Don't I know you?

Rachel I ... I don't think so... (*She turns away to hide her face*)

Procter runs around her to get another look at her face

Procter Yes! Of course!

Rachel (*alarmed*) What?

Procter Mrs Parker!

Rachel Er … well…

Procter I never forget a face. In the SAS we were trained never to forget a face.

Rachel Couldn't you make an exception in my case?

Procter You live at number ten!

Rachel D-do I?

Procter But you're not at number ten *now*, are you?

Rachel Aren't I?

Procter This isn't number ten.

Rachel Isn't it?

Procter (*proudly*) This—is number thirty-five!

Rachel Is it?

He holds his notebook out to her

Procter See? Mrs Brent—thirty-five.

Rachel No wonder I couldn't work the video.

Procter (*suspicion dawning*) Oh dear, oh dear. I have another thought…

Rachel Well, please don't! Just collect your dog and continue your walk. (*She tries to urge him on his way*)

Procter Perhaps *you* are the intruder?

Rachel No, no!

Procter You live at number ten but you have broken into number thirty-five. Is that the scenario?

Rachel Certainly not!

Procter I shall have to search for signs of a forced entry.

Rachel You won't find any!

Procter I'd better call the police. (*He takes out his mobile telephone*)

Rachel No!

Procter (*reasonably*) You can't go around breaking into people's houses, Mrs Parker.

Rachel I didn't! (*She grabs his arm, trying to restrain him*)

Procter Have a care, madam. My dog's outside. I only have to whistle and he'll have that door down in sixty seconds.

Rachel (*desperately*) I'm babysitting!

Procter Babysitting?'

Rachel *House*-sitting! Yes! That's what I'm doing! I'm house-sitting for Mrs Brent. She's not in, so I'm house-sitting. There's been a spate of burglaries around here lately.

Procter Yes, I know! Why do you think I'm on my toes? (*He demonstrates*) You're very smartly dressed for house-sitting.

Rachel Oh, it's nothing—I picked it up from Oxfam! I'm a great supporter of the Third World.

Whereupon Frank bursts in from the bedroom, wearing brightly-coloured boxer shorts and a blue vest

Frank I think I'm ready now!

Procter and Rachel stare at him in surprise. Frank sees Procter and freezes in horror. Procter, fearing the worst, throws himself upon the intruder and wrestles him to the ground. Frank is alarmed by this unexpected turn of events. Rachel stares at the writhing figures, appalled

Rachel No! No! Let go of him!

Procter stops struggling, but retains his firm hold on Frank as he looks up from the floor at Rachel

Procter You *know* this person in shorts?
Rachel Of course I know him!
Procter And he's *not* a burglar?
Rachel Of course he's not a burglar!
Procter (*sagely*) Well, you can never be sure.

He releases Frank, and they both get up from the floor. Procter tidies up his clothes and looks in surprise at Frank's mode of dress. Frank shifts, nervously

Frank You're … you're not her *husband*, are you?
Rachel Of course he's not my husband!
Frank (*quietly*) Thank God for that…!
Rachel He was just walking his dog.
Procter You've heard of Neighbourhood Watch?
Frank Yes…
Procter Well, I'm watching. (*He watches Frank, belligerently*)
Rachel His name's Procter.
Frank The dog?
Rachel *Him!*
Frank Oh.

Procter moves to Rachel, suspiciously

Procter So, Mrs Parker—you're spending the evening in somebody else's house in the company of a strange man in his underwear?

Rachel He's not a strange man.

Procter He is to me! (*He glares at the strange man, critically*)

Frank (*finding his courage*) You've no right to come in here asking questions!

Procter In Neighbourhood Watch we work closely with the police.

Frank (*nervous again*) Do you?

Procter Oh, yes. (*Returning to Frank*) I'm sure my friend Constable Weaver would be very interested in what I've seen here tonight…

Frank You wouldn't tell him!

Procter I might…

Frank sinks into the armchair, despondently. Rachel hastily collects the plate of "bits" and proffers them to Procter

Rachel Would you like a sausage?

Procter I hope you're not trying to bribe me.

Rachel With a sausage?

Procter Where did they come from?

Frank *I* cooked them.

Procter looks at him with dark suspicion

Procter *You?*

Frank (*with a modest shrug*) Just a few little bits…

Rachel I can recommend the fishy things.

Procter (*taking one*) Do you always cook "little bits" in your underwear? (*He pops the mini vol-au-vent into his mouth*)

Frank Well … it's so hot in the kitchen.

Procter is surprisingly appreciative of the mini vol-au-vent

Procter H'm. Very nice. (*To Rachel*) Does Mrs Brent know that you're house-sitting in the company of a half-naked cook?

Rachel Yes, of course.

Procter (*astonished*) And she doesn't mind?

Rachel No.

Procter looks from one to the other, heavily suspicious

Procter Do I sense vice? There seems to be an aura of lust in the air.

Rachel That'll be the vol-au-vents.

Procter Have I, by any chance, stumbled upon a den of iniquity?

Rachel No, of course not! There's a perfectly simple explanation.

Frank Is there?

Procter (*turning to Frank, imperiously*) Ready for *what*?

Frank has temporarily lost track of the conversation

Frank Sorry?
Procter Just now when you surprised us with your sudden unexpected appearance you called out "I think I'm ready now!"
Frank D-did I?
Procter In the SAS we're trained to remember what people say.
Frank (*to Rachel*) The SAS?
Rachel He used to be in the SAS.
Frank He might have killed me...!
Procter (*the voice of doom*) Ready for *what*?
Frank Well ... er...

Rachel comes to the rescue

Rachel Jogging!
Procter Jogging?
Frank (*appalled*) Jogging?!
Rachel You must have seen people jogging. They're always at it round here. (*She demonstrates*) One, two! One, two! One, two! He was just changing when you arrived.
Procter (*to Frank*) Is this true? You were about to go jogging?
Frank Well ... er ... yes.
Procter Cook your "little bits" and then go jogging?
Frank Yes!
Procter Do you always jog on a full stomach?
Rachel Oh, *he* hasn't had any!
Procter Sorry?
Rachel Little bits. He cooked them for *me*. Wasn't that kind? Are you *sure* you wouldn't like one, Mr Procter? (*She thrusts the plate of bits at him*)
Procter Don't think you can seduce me with a small sausage.
Frank (*rising, hopefully*) So that's all right, then, isn't it?
Procter What's all right, then?
Frank Now you know what I'm doing here. So there's nothing for you to worry about.
Procter (*reluctantly*) H'm ... I suppose if it's all right with Mrs Brent it'll *have* to be all right with me...
Rachel So now you and your dog can carry on walking.
Procter Right! (*He turns to Frank, abruptly*) Off you go, then!
Frank Sorry?
Procter Don't let me detain you. I can see you're anxious to be on your way. You're poised on your toes like a beagle.

Frank What?

Procter Jogging! (*He demonstrates*) One, two! One, two! One, two!

Frank I thought perhaps I'd start later…

Procter (*pushing him towards the door*) You can't hang around here dressed like that!

Rachel Yes—on your way, Frank!

Frank What?!

Rachel Well, you wouldn't want Mr Procter to think that you weren't *really* going jogging, now would you?

Frank No fear…!

Rachel So off you go! One, two! One, two! One, two!

Frank Oh, my God…!

Frank opens the door and races out into the night, the dog barking excitedly as he goes

Procter I'm afraid he's rather excitable.

Rachel Well, he's not used to people watching him when he's jogging.

Procter The dog!

Rachel Oh—yes.

Procter I'll leave you, then, to enjoy your … "little bits". (*He goes towards the front door*)

Rachel (*politely*) Thank you for calling, Mr Procter.

Procter All part of the service!

Procter goes, closing the door behind him, his dog barking as they go off down the road

Rachel sighs, wearily, and takes the plate of "bits" into the kitchen, eating comfort food despondently

The Lights fade to Black-out

The Lights come up on Victor's and Rachel's house

Victor comes in from the kitchen, leading Georgina by the hand. She holds back

Victor What's the matter?

Georgina Where are we going?

Victor Where do you think? We don't want to waste any *more* time, do we? (*Seeing her lack of enthusiasm*) What's the matter? You've had a whole bar of Cadbury's Fruit and Nut, you must be in the mood by now!

Georgina Fruit and Nut's hardly romantic, is it? Smoked salmon would have
been better…

Victor I'll remember next time. (*He starts to go*) Come on—through here!

Georgina What's through there?

Victor (*trying to be patient*) The hall—and the stairs.

Georgina Do the stairs lead to the bedrooms?

Victor Yes, of course!

Georgina That's what I thought…

Victor Come on, then!

Victor grins and goes into the hall, leaving the door slightly ajar

*Georgina hesitates, uncertainly. She goes to check her appearance in the
mirror, takes a comb out of her evening bag and does a few very small
adjustments to her coiffure. She replaces the comb in her handbag and tries
to pluck up courage. She is about to follow Victor when——*

The doorbell rings

*Georgina freezes in horror for a moment, then whispers in a small, frightened
voice*

Georgina Victor…

Again the doorbell rings

*Georgina leaves her handbag on the crescent table above the kitchen door
and edges nearer to the open door to the hall. She whispers again with a little
more urgency*

Victor…!

*Victor walks in from the hall. He has now taken off his trousers and tie and
his shirt is hanging loosely over his bare legs. He stares at her in alarm*

Victor (*whispering urgently*) There's someone at the door!

Georgina Yes!

Victor Who is it?

Georgina How do *I* know?!

Victor Well, whoever it is they mustn't find *you* here! Go and hide upstairs!

*Victor pushes Georgina out into the hall, unceremoniously, and closes the
door*

The doorbell rings again

Victor is about to open the front door when he realizes that he is without his trousers. He looks about, then quickly picks up a tartan rug and wraps it around his waist like a kilt. He opens the door, carefully concealing his kilted lower half behind it

    Henry is there. He is a good-looking man in his fifties, dressed in casuals, actor style

Victor stares at him in horror

    Henry!!
Henry Yes.
Victor You don't live here! You live at number thirty-five!
Henry (*surprised by his vehemence*) Yes. I know.
Victor You're not usually home at this time!
Henry (*patiently*) Victor … can I come in?
Victor Is it urgent?
Henry Yes. As a matter of fact it is.
Victor Oh. Right.

Henry comes into the room. Victor remains with the door still open to hide his nether regions. Henry turns back and sees the extraordinary sight of Victor hiding behind the door

Henry Aren't you going to shut the door?
Victor Are you staying, then?
Henry For a minute or two, yes. Is that a problem?
Victor No. No, that'll be fine…
Henry Shut the door then! (*He sits on the sofa*)

Victor shuts the door and moves down into the room, deeply embarrassed by his attire. Henry is facing the other way and does not yet see him

    I was lucky to catch you in.
Victor Yes…

A pause

Henry You might have been out.
Victor Yes…

A pause

Henry Down the pub.
Victor Yes...

A pause

Henry But you're not.
Victor No...

A pause

Henry So it's my lucky night.
Victor (*quietly*) I wish it was mine...!
Henry (*turning*) The thing is, Victor— (*He sees Victor in the tartan rug*)

Victor shifts, embarrassed. After a moment he starts to execute a modest Scottish dance, then gives up in despair and sits beside Henry on the sofa. He has the greatest difficulty retaining his modesty, unused as he is to Scottish costume

Victor Look, is this going to take very long? I was just going out.
Henry Dressed like that?
Victor Ah. Yes. I ... I'd taken my trousers off, you see.
Henry Any particular reason?
Victor I was going to press them.
Henry Press your trousers?
Victor Yes. They needed pressing. So I was going to do it.
Henry And *then* go out?
Victor Oh, yes. After I'd pressed them. I ... I wasn't expecting you, you see.
Henry No. You wouldn't be.

Victor speaks loudly for the sake of the hidden Rachel

Victor Henry—you're an actor, for heaven's sake!
Henry (*puzzled*) Yes...
Victor A *very—successful—actor—Henry*!
Henry Thank you. (*Puzzled*) Do you want my autograph?
Victor Not at the moment. I've got other things on my mind.
Henry Like pressing your trousers?
Victor Yes...
Henry (*suddenly*) Has Georgina been here tonight?
Victor What? No! Never! Why?
Henry (*pointing*) Well, that looks like her handbag over there.

Victor leaps up and hastens across to pick up Georgina's handbag, almost losing his tartan rug in the process. He grabs the bag and hides it under his arms

Victor No—no, this is Rachel's! Definitely Rachel's. She's always leaving it lying about.
Henry What a coincidence. Georgina's got one just like it.
Victor Has she really? Good Lord! That shows how common they are. Everybody's got one. I'll buy Rachel another! (*He casts the handbag, disdainfully, into the wastepaper basket*)

Henry is rather surprised by this cavalier attitude to a harmless handbag. Victor returns to him, clutching the tartan rug

I thought you were in a play at the theatre?
Henry Yes. I am.
Victor (*wildly*) Well, why aren't you out there doing it? You've no right to be back here!
Henry The safety curtain stuck.
Victor (*blankly*) Sorry?
Henry The iron safety curtain. It goes up and down. They got it down but they couldn't get it up. So they sent us all home.
Victor Sent you home because they couldn't get it up?
Henry Yes.
Victor (*agressively*) Couldn't you do the play with the safety curtain *down*?
Henry No point if the audience couldn't see us. And we couldn't get another five hundred people on to the stage.
Victor No, I suppose not. Would be a bit crowded.
Henry So they sent us all home.
Victor And you came to visit me? Well, it's very nice of you—any other night would have been fine—but tonight I do have an alternative arrangement. So if—if you could just—you know— (*He tries to urge Henry on his way*)
Henry Oh, I'm not here to socialise.
Victor (*nervously*) You're not?
Henry Oh, no. It's quite a serious matter.
Victor Is it?
Henry Oh, yes.
Victor How serious?
Henry Very serious.
Victor Matter of life and death?
Henry Could be.
Victor Good Lord…!
Henry (*laughing suddenly*) It's funny you being here without your trousers on.

Victor Is it? Oh, good. (*Puzzled*) Is the play you're *in* a comedy?
Henry I saw a man in the street!
Victor Well, there are a few of them about at this time.
Henry A man in the street without his trousers! Just like you! Ha! Ha! Ha!
Victor (*appalled*) A man in this street without his trousers?
Henry Yes. Just now as I got out of the taxi. Coloured shorts and a blue vest.
   Going like the clappers.
Victor Really? Good Lord. (*Puzzled*) Is that what you came here to tell me?
Henry Oh, no. No. I... I'm afraid I've done rather a stupid thing.
Victor (*quietly*) So have I...!
Henry I left my latchkey behind.
Victor Your latchkey?
Henry Yes. You know—the—er— (*He mimes turning a latchkey*)
Victor Ah! To your front door?
Henry Yes.
Victor Left it behind in the theatre?
Henry No. Left it behind at home.
Victor At number thirty-five?
Henry Yes. This afternoon when I left. So I can't get in. Georgina's not there,
   you see.
Victor No, I know she isn't...!
Henry *How* do you know?
Victor You just said so.
Henry So I can't get in.
Victor To number thirty-five?
Henry Yes. On account of—er— (*He mimes the latchkey again*) So that's
   why I'm here.
Victor (*puzzled*) Is that a solution?
Henry I hope so! Don't tell me Georgina didn't give it to you?
Victor (*lost for a moment*) Sorry?
Henry I thought it was the usual procedure.
Victor (*with a nervous laugh*) Usual procedure?
Henry Well, it's very convenient for *me*, isn't it?
Victor Is it?
Henry Of course! If I come home unexpectedly—like tonight—and I can't
   get in, I know where she's left it, don't I?
Victor Left it?
Henry The spare key!
Victor Oh, I *see*! No.
Henry No what?
Victor No spare key. Not that I know of.
Henry Perhaps Rachel knows?
Victor Sorry?

Henry Where the spare key is. Women usually know about things like that.
(*A sudden thought*) Ah! Perhaps it's in her handbag! (*He sets off towards
the wastepaper basket*)

Victor No!! (*He races Henry to the wastepaper basket, dropping his tartan
rug in the process*) I—I don't like prying into ladies' handbags! You never
know what you'll find.

Henry Well, *I* don't mind! Give it to me. *I*'ll look.

Victor No! No—it's *my* wife's! If anybody's going to look *I*'ll look!

Henry Get on with it, then!

*Victor delves into the wastepaper basket, turns away from Henry, opens the
handbag and looks inside*

Victor (*quietly*) Good heavens, I didn't know she'd got one of those…

Henry *Well?*

Victor No! No key! What did I tell you? (*He casts the handbag back into the
wastepaper basket and retrieves his tartan rug*)

Henry Are you expecting Rachel back *soon*?

Victor I hope not…!

Henry What?

Victor I *think* not! She's at the boathouse. She's taken up rowing, you see.
(*He mimes rowing and almost loses his tartan rug again*)

Henry So you're here all on your own?

Victor (*wildly*) Of course I'm all on my own! That's why I'm going out! I
can't stand being alone.

Henry Perhaps I'd better catch her at the boathouse, then.

Victor (*delighted*) What a good idea. You'll definitely catch her there. If not,
she'll be in the Pizza Hut.

Henry That key's supposed to be *here* in case of an emergency!

Victor (*quietly*) And this is certainly that…!

Henry We could search your house. (*He starts to move*)

Victor No!

Henry What?

Victor We'd never find it.

Henry We could try.

Victor We'd fail!

Henry You can't be sure. It's probably in your bedroom. (*He sets off towards
the bedroom*)

Victor (*pursuing him*) No! No—much better if you go and catch Rachel at
the boathouse! (*He pushes him towards the front door*) For all we know she
may have the key *with* her.

Henry Why should she have the key to *my* house with her when she goes
rowing?

Victor *I* don't know! For safe keeping? Anyway, if she hasn't got it with her she can tell you where it is. (*He opens the door*)
Henry Of course! Then I can come back here and get it.
Victor (*doubtfully*) Yes...

Henry starts to go

Just don't do all that too quickly...

Henry turns back at the door with a big grin

Henry I should put your trousers on before Rachel gets back.

Henry goes, happily

Victor closes the door and runs across to call into the hall

Victor It's all right—he's gone!

No response. He looks puzzled

Georgina!

Still nothing

Victor goes into the hall and returns almost immediately

Where the hell has she got to?

Black-out

The Lights come up on Henry's and Georgina's house. Someone is knocking on the front door

Rachel runs in from the kitchen, anxiously, and opens the door

Frank staggers in, exhausted

Frank Has he gone?
Rachel Who?
Frank The SAS!
Rachel Oh. Yes.
Frank Thank God for that! (*He collapses on to the sofa*) That damn dog chased me halfway down the path!

Rachel I expect he was trying to be friendly.
Frank Friendly? He was like the Hound of the Baskervilles!
Rachel Anyway, he's gone now.

Rachel darts out into the kitchen

Frank massages his sore feet

Frank (*calling*) Do you think he'll come back?
Rachel (*off*) The Hound of the Baskervilles?
Frank No—Mr Procter!
Rachel (*off*) I hope not!

Rachel returns from the kitchen with a bottle of wine and two glasses, smiling at him with revived optimism

Frank, still trying to gather his breath, sees her romantic look and watches her approach with apprehension. Rachel puts the glasses down on the sofa table and pours the wine

(*With happy innuendo*) So that's all right, then, isn't it?
Frank Sorry?
Rachel Now there's just the *two* of us again…
Frank Ah … yes.
Rachel (*sitting beside him*) So we can carry on from where we left off.
Frank (*not too keen*) Can we?

Rachel hands him a glass of wine and smiles, encouragingly

Rachel Happy anniversary…
Frank Sorry?
Rachel Three weeks… Remember? (*She raises her glass*)
Frank Oh—yes…

They drink, he half-heartedly, she enthusiastically. Then she puts down their glasses on the sofa table and moves a little closer, bringing her face nearer to his and gazing into his eyes. A moment

I wonder if there are any little bits left?

Rachel moves away from him, abruptly

Rachel How can you think of food at a time like this?

Frank I'm hungry! I've been jogging!

A sudden noise from upstairs. Grateful for the excuse, Rachel throws herself into his arms and clings on

Rachel There's somebody upstairs! It may be a burglar! Go and find Mr Procter!
Frank I'd sooner face the burglar.
Henry (*off*) Hullo? Is somebody there?
Rachel Oh, my God—it's Henry!

They leap up in panic. Rachel runs around the sofa to pick up her discarded track-suit

Frank Who's Henry?
Rachel Georgina's husband!

Frank races to join her

Frank What's he doing *here*?
Rachel He *lives* here!
Frank Yes, but he wasn't supposed to *be* here!

Rachel is about to put on her track-suit trousers, realizes that there is no time and quickly shoves the track-suit under the sofa

Henry comes in from upstairs and sees them. Naturally, he is extremely surprised

Henry Rachel!
Rachel Henry!

Henry looks at Frank, inquiringly

Frank (*weakly*) Frank...
Henry I *thought* I heard voices. (*He looks at them, suspiciously*) Well? Is anyone going to tell me what this is all about?
Rachel Now Henry—I know what you must be thinking——
Henry And you're right!
Rachel Well, you're wrong.
Henry I hope so!
Rachel How did you get upstairs?
Henry The bedroom window was open. I've been looking for you at the boathouse.

Rachel W-wasn't I there?

Henry No, you weren't! You weren't at the Pizza Hut, either. And the one place I *didn't* expect to find you was in *my* house in the company of a young man in his underwear. (*Looking at Frank*) Haven't I seen you somewhere before?

Rachel (*trying to carry it off*) Henry, I know it looks awful. Suspicious even. But there's a perfectly reasonable explanation.

Frank Is there?

Rachel (*going to him*) Of course there is! Off you go, then!

Frank Sorry?

Rachel I've given you some money, so now you must carry on running and call at the *other* houses. (*She opens the front door*)

Frank (*appalled*) What?!

Rachel Go on! Off you go! One, two! One, two! One, two!

Frank But I—I— Oh, my God…!

Frank runs out into the night

Rachel closes the door and returns to Henry

Rachel He's doing a charity run for the Boy Scouts.

Henry (*remembering*) Ah—that's where I saw him! Running down the street like the clappers.

Rachel I think people are wonderful who do work like that, don't you?

Henry He looks half dead. (*He settles on the sofa*)

Rachel I expect he's a little out of practice. But it's the spirit that counts, isn't it? You are silly, Henry. You should have rung the doorbell. I'd have let you in.

Henry Well, I didn't expect *you* to be here.

Rachel Didn't you have your key?

Henry No. That's the point. I left it here when I went to the theatre.

Rachel Well, why aren't you *at* the theatre?

Henry They cancelled the performance.

Rachel (*concerned*) Good heavens, had somebody died?

Henry No, no. They couldn't raise the safety curtain, so they sent us home.

Rachel But why did you go looking for me at the boathouse?

Henry To get the spare key, of course.

Rachel (*warily*) Spare key?

Henry You've got our spare key, haven't you?

Rachel Well … yes. But I didn't think you knew.

Henry Of course I knew! Georgina *told* me she gave it to you.

Rachel Why on earth did she tell you that?

Henry (*puzzled*) Well, I had to *know*, didn't I?

Rachel I didn't think you knew anything about it.
Henry Why? It's no big deal, is it?
Rachel (*escaping below him*) Well—as it happens—no. But it might have
been. When did she tell you?
Henry I don't remember. Does it matter? About two months ago.
Rachel Two months? Three weeks!
Henry Sorry?
Rachel I can't believe she told you about it.
Henry Well, it's only natural, isn't it? Everybody does it.
Rachel Do they?
Henry Of course. Everyone leaves a spare key with a neighbour in case of
emergency.
Rachel What sort of emergency?
Henry (*patiently*) Like me forgetting my own key and not being able to get
in. I went to *your* house first, of course.
Rachel Did you?
Henry Yes. Had a word with Victor. I was lucky to catch him in, as a matter
of fact.
Rachel Really?
Henry Yes. He was just going out. (*He laughs*) I caught him without any
trousers!
Rachel Where on earth was he going without any trousers?
Henry I don't know. Scottish dancing, I think.

Rachel looks puzzled

Rachel Scottish dancing?
Henry I expect you were hoping to find Georgina here?
Rachel Georgina? (*Grateful for the suggestion*) Ah—yes! That's right! I
was!
Henry But she wasn't.
Rachel No.
Henry She told me she was going to the pictures with a girlfriend tonight.
Rachel (*innocently*) Well, I expect she did. She's very fond of the pictures.
Henry So why is there a bottle of wine and two glasses on the table?

Rachel runs around to look at the bottle of wine in horror

Rachel What?! Ah—yes— I … gave a glass to the charity runner!
Henry (*doubtfully*) Oh, yes?
Rachel I felt so sorry for him. Poor man, he was exhausted.
Henry I could tell.
Rachel So I gave him a glass. I knew you wouldn't mind. He was very
grateful.

Henry I'm sure he was. If he gets a glass of wine in every house he stops at, his feet'll never touch the ground. So … so *you* had one to keep him company?

Rachel Well, I couldn't let him drink alone, could I? It would seem so rude.

Henry You found the bottle opener all right, then? Sometimes I have to search for hours.

Rachel Oh—yes—thank you. (*Anxious to go*) Well, I—I'd better be off—!

Henry (*deep in thought*) Rachel…

Rachel Y-yes?

Henry I know this is silly of me, but I … I'm a bit confused…

Rachel C-confused?

Henry Just a bit, yes. You … you came round here from the boathouse … after your rowing?

Rachel Er … yes.

Henry Well, that's what I find confusing. Do you … do you *always* dress like that when you go rowing——

Rachel tries to carry it off with a smile

Rachel I *knew* you'd be wondering!

Henry I am.

Rachel Well, there's a perfectly reasonable explanation.

Henry I thought there might be…!

Rachel (*needing Dutch courage*) Could I have another glass of wine?

Henry Help yourself.

Rachel Thank you. (*She helps herself*) Would *you* like one?

Henry No, thanks. I think I'd better keep my wits about me for this. (*He remains seated, waiting for the exposition*)

Rachel takes a generous sip of wine and sits beside him before beginning

Rachel Well… I… I was rowing, you see.

Henry Yes. I know.

Rachel In a boat.

Henry That would help.

Rachel On the river.

Henry It was a lovely evening for it.

Rachel Yes, it was, wasn't it?

Henry Ideal for rowing.

Rachel Yes.

Henry You couldn't have chosen a better time.

Rachel Exactly. So there I was.

Henry On the river.

Rachel Yes. Going quite quickly, as a matter of fact.
Henry I didn't know you *could* go quickly in those things.
Rachel Oh, yes. And I've only been doing it for three weeks.
Henry You're obviously a quick learner.
Rachel Yes. (*She gets up to take another generous helping of wine before resuming her seat*)
Henry So there you were, rowing down the river...
Rachel Yes. And ... and that's when it happened.
Henry What happened?
Rachel The storm broke.
Henry Storm?
Rachel Yes.
Henry I thought it was a lovely evening.
Rachel It was. Until the storm broke.
Henry I didn't know there'd been a storm tonight. I never heard anything.
Rachel Well ... perhaps more of a squall.
Henry Ah! A sudden squall?
Rachel Yes. Very sudden.
Henry I can imagine. As you were— (*he mimes rowing*) rowing along?
Rachel Yes. It suddenly hit me with full force. And, after all, I've only been doing it for three weeks. I'm not very experienced.
Henry Even though you are a quick learner.
Rachel Exactly. So ... so that's how I ended up *in* the river instead of *on* it.

Henry gazes at her in horror

Henry You capsized?!
Rachel Yes!
Henry Good Lord... (*He pauses*) Lucky you're a strong swimmer.
Rachel Oh, yes. I was in no danger.
Henry That is a relief. What about the boat?
Rachel Sorry?
Henry The boat you were in at the time. Or is that still floating down the river?
Rachel Oh, no. They got it back all right.
Henry Oh, good!
Rachel So there I was—soaked to the skin.
Henry You would be.

Rachel prepares to deliver the coup de grâce

Rachel And then suddenly I remembered that I'd got *your* spare key in my handbag! (*She smiles, triumphantly*)

Henry Didn't you have a key to your own house?

Rachel No. Victor had lost *his*—so he'd borrowed mine. Otherwise I'd have gone straight home, wouldn't I?

Henry So you came back here to dry off?

Rachel Yes.

Henry ponders, deeply

Henry You'll have to speak to the committee…

Rachel Sorry?

Henry Well, they'll have to improve the facilities at the club if when you fall in the river you have to dry off in a private house.

Rachel (*smiling, the brave heroine*) I knew you wouldn't mind.

Henry We wouldn't want you catching your death of cold, would we?

Rachel takes a final sip of wine

Rachel So that's how I came to be wearing one of Georgina's dresses.

Henry stares at her in surprise

I'd nothing to change into, you see. So I borrowed this from Georgina.

Henry (*peering at it*) I don't think I've seen that one before.

Rachel I expect it's new! You know what Georgina's like about shops. And, after all, you are a successful actor, so you can afford it. (*She hastily collects her sports bag and prepares to leave*) Right! I'll leave you to it, then. (*She starts to go*)

Henry (*going to her, thoughtfully*) Rachel…

Rachel (*hesitating*) Y-yes?

Henry Aren't you going to give it to me before you go?

Rachel Sorry?

Henry The spare key.

Rachel Ah—yes—now where did he put it? (*Quickly correcting herself*) Er—where did I put it? Oh, dear, I can't remember…

Henry Well, once you'd got in through the front door, presumably you put it down *some*where?

Rachel (*flustered*) I was wet! I'd fallen in the river! I wasn't concentrating on keys!

Henry (*amused*) All right. Never mind. I'm inside now, so it doesn't matter. I expect you'll remember tomorrow.

Rachel Yes, I expect I will…! (*She opens the door, anxious to be gone*)

Henry Rachel…

Rachel Y-yes?

Henry Don't forget to let Georgina have her dress back. (*He laughs*)
Rachel Ah—no! Right!

Rachel stumbles out, closing the door behind her

*Henry shakes his head with a bemused smile, picks up the bottle and the
two glasses and goes into the kitchen as——*

The Lights fade to Black-out

*The Lights come up on Victor's and Rachel's house. Someone is outside,
ringing the doorbell*

*Victor comes in from the bedroom. He has now got his trousers back on.
He goes and opens the door, hopefully*

Procter is there, his unseen dog pulling at the leash and barking

Victor What do *you* want?
Procter I'm here to help. May I come in?
Victor You're not coming in with that dog!
Procter He'll stay outside.
Victor He'd better!
Procter (*to the dog*) Now stay, boy, stay… Good boy. Good boy. (*He casts
the leash aside and comes in*)

*Victor closes the door on the dog and follows Procter into the room,
impatiently*

Victor All right—what's it all about?
Procter I'm Mr Procter.
Victor Is that of any interest?
Procter (*smiling*) It is to *Mrs* Procter! I'm a member of Neighbourhood
Watch.
Victor (*uninterested*) Oh, yes…?
Procter We keep a watch on what's going on.
Victor Yes. I bet you do…!
Procter And there's a *lot* going on tonight, I can tell you.
Victor (*guiltily*) There's nothing going on here!
Procter There's a man outside jogging in his underwear, for starters!
Victor Oh, *you* saw him, too? I must have a look at that. (*He goes to look out
of the window*)

Procter sits down, making himself at home

Procter Now, sir—I suspect that you may have been the victim of a burglary.

Victor turns from the window and is surprised to see his visitor sitting down. He goes to him

Victor What makes you suspect that?

Procter I saw an intruder making her escape.

Victor A *lady* intruder?

Procter Yes. Through an open window, down a drainpipe and away. *She* was going in one direction, the jogger in the other. It was a fascinating sight.

Victor It must have been. Did you … recognize her?

Procter No. She was too quick for me.

Victor (*quietly*) Thank God for that…!

Procter However, I have alerted Constable Weaver on my mobile. (*He produces his mobile telephone and brandishes it*)

Victor You told the police?!

Procter Of course. No point in Neighbourhood Watch watching neighbours and not reporting possible offenders.

Victor Look, I think you must be mistaken. I've been in all evening. If I'd been burgled I'd have known, and I can assure you there's no sign of a break-in.

Procter puts away his mobile, gets up from the sofa and wanders a little, thinking deeply

Procter I see… In that case perhaps there's some *other* reason for the hasty departure of a young lady down your drainpipe?

Victor What are you suggesting?

Procter (*with a world-weary shrug*) I'm a man of the world, sir. It happens all the time.

Victor (*rather hurt*) Not *all* the time. (*Hastily denying it*) Not to *me* at *all*! So you'd better get on your mobile and tell Constable Weaver it was all a mistake!

Procter Oh, I can't do that, sir. Once the wheels of Weaver have been set in motion there's no stopping them. And I've already made a note in my Filofax. (*He notices something*) Did you know that there's a lady's handbag in your wastepaper basket?

Victor stares at him, blankly, for a second

Victor What? (*He activates himself and races across to pick up the wastepaper basket, clutching it to him protectingly, pushing Procter aside in the process. He looks down into it*) Good Lord, *there* it is!

Procter Sorry?

Victor I've been looking for that all the evening. And there it was all the time. Well, well, well!

Procter Funny place to keep a handbag... (*He drifts away to resume his seat*)

Victor Yes. Yes, it is, isn't it?

Procter Does your wife keep all her handbags in various wastepaper baskets throughout the house?

Victor (*still clutching the wastepaper basket*) No, no! Of course not. No— er— (*thinking hard*) as a matter of tact, Mr—er—?

Procter Procter.

Victor Mr Procter, my wife and I have been... (*with an embarrassed smile*) playing games tonight.

Procter (*instantly suspicious*) What sort of games would that be, sir?

Victor Hide and seek.

Procter Hide and seek?!

Victor Yes. I... I close my eyes and count to ten, and she ... she hides something. Just something small—you know. Then I have to look for it. (*He puts the wastepaper basket down at the end of the sofa*)

Procter How long does she give you to look for it?

Victor How long? Ah—well, it varies really. There's no hard and fast rule about it.

Procter You mean you go on looking until you find it? Or until you give up?

Victor Yes. They're fairly loose house rules.

Procter (*profoundly*) Presumably there was no time limit on the handbag round?

Victor stares at him, blankly, for a second

Victor Sorry?

Procter Well—you were still looking, presumably, when I found what I found in the wastepaper basket?

Victor Ah! Yes! Yes, I suppose I was. (*He takes Procter's arm and steers him gently towards the front door*) So, you see, Mr—er—?

Procter Procter!

Victor Mr Procter—though it might have been fairly exciting out there on the streets tonight, in the quiet of our homes it has all been remarkably ordinary.

Procter Apart from the possible lady intruder...

Victor Sorry?

Procter Down the—er——

Victor Drainpipe?

Procter Yes.

Victor Ah. That. Yes. Well... (*his mind racing*) now this is going to sound very silly to a man in your position, Mr—er—?

Procter Procter!!

Victor Mr Procter—a man in your position with a dog and both feet on the ground, but our game of hide-and-seek did go a little further tonight.

Procter (*suspiciously*) How *much* further?

Victor Well— (*pretending to be amused*) you see, in the last round of the game—just before you arrived, as a matter of fact—my wife—and you're going to find this very difficult to believe—my wife decided to hide *herself*!

Procter (*glazed*) Hide *herself*…?

Victor I knew you'd be surprised. Anyway, she must have been cheating!

Procter Cheating…?

Victor Yes. No wonder I couldn't find her! You see, the game was supposed to be confined to this house, but she must have climbed out of the bedroom window and disappeared down the road!

Procter considers this for a moment

Procter You're … you're sure it was your *wife*, sir?

Victor (*laughing*) Of course I'm sure! I do know what my own wife looks like! So you'd better tell Constable Weaver that it was all a mistake.

Procter Well, I would, sir. I would do that. The only trouble is—tonight your wife has been house-sitting at number thirty-five.

Procter goes, his dog barking noisily, he remonstrating with it

Victor closes the door, deeply puzzled, and moves towards the hall as the Lights fade to Black-out

The Lights come up on Henry's and Georgina's house

The front door opens and Georgina comes in, furtively, uncertain whether Henry is there or not

Realizing that she is a little over-dressed for having been to the cinema, she hastily takes her dress off. She takes a shirt and slacks out of a cupboard drawer, puts on the shirt and is about to put on the slacks

Henry comes in and sees her

Georgina overdoes her surprise

Georgina Henry!

Henry Good heavens—what a welcome! I come home early and you start taking your clothes off.

Georgina I—I didn't know *you* were here!

Henry Who were you expecting, then? The window-cleaner? (*He laughs*)

Georgina I was just slipping into something casual. (*She fastens up her slacks*)

Henry You mean you'd been all dressed up just to go to the cinema?

Georgina No, no! No—I just got a bit hot running home.

Henry Running?

Georgina (*quickly*) Walking! Walking home. (*She shoves her dress untidily into the drawer and closes it*)

Henry Must have been a very short film.

Georgina Sorry?

Henry Just a cartoon, possibly?

Georgina No, no—but I'd seen it before. (*She changes the subject and assumes surprise*) Shouldn't you be at the theatre?

Henry They cancelled the performance. So I came home and surprised everyone. Like a drink?

Georgina (*gratefully*) Oh, yes, please…!

Henry Yes. I expect you're ready for one after walking all the way home and changing your clothes. (*He sees to the drinks*) You'll never guess what's been happening tonight!

Georgina (*quietly*) Neither will *you*…!

Henry (*laughing*) I had to climb through a window!

Georgina *You* did? (*She laughs, amused by the coincidence, then quickly sets her face*) You *did*? Why?

Henry I'd left my key behind, so I popped in on Victor to see if he'd got our spare one.

Georgina And … and had he?

Henry No. That's why I had to climb in through the window. (*He arrives with the drinks*)

Georgina Thanks. (*She takes one and sits on the sofa*)

Henry Cheers!

Georgina Cheers!

They drink. Henry chuckles

Henry Victor was behaving very strangely tonight.

Georgina chokes on her drink

Georgina R-really? In what way?

Henry When he opened the door he didn't have any trousers on!

Georgina What?!

Henry And he had a tartan rug wrapped around his waist.

Georgina W-why?
Henry I don't know. Said he was pressing his trousers. But *I* think he had a woman in there.

Georgina chokes again

Georgina Victor? Don't be silly! Victor wouldn't do that.
Henry That's what *I* thought. But either he had a woman in there or he's in need of counselling. By the way, Rachel borrowed one of your dresses.
Georgina (*surprised*) One of mine?
Henry Yes. After she fell in the river. (*He sits beside her and enjoys his drink*)

Georgina is completely bewildered

Georgina You … you've *seen* Rachel, then?
Henry Yes. She was here when I climbed in through the window.
Georgina Oh… Look—I can explain——
Henry You? There's nothing for *you* to explain.
Georgina Isn't there? Oh, good…! Rachel must have been very surprised to see you.
Henry She certainly was!
Georgina H-h-how did she get in?
Henry With our spare key, of course! You gave it to her, didn't you?
Georgina Ah, yes—of course I did! There was a good reason for that…
Henry I know!
Georgina Do you?
Henry Well, she has to have our spare key in case of emergency, doesn't she?
Georgina Ah—yes—of course.
Henry Unfortunately, I missed her at the boathouse.
Georgina Sorry?
Henry She'd taken the key with her to the boathouse, but by the time I'd got there she'd gone.
Georgina (*pretending to be puzzled*) But … what was she doing *here*?
Henry Came back to dry off after she fell in the river. That's when she changed into one of your dresses.
Georgina Could I have another gin?
Henry (*surprised by her speedy consumption*) Coming up. (*He takes her glass and goes to refill it*)

Georgina has no idea what has been really happening

    And another thing—!
Georgina Don't say there's something *else*!

Henry Oh, yes. This is the best bit. (*He chuckles, gleefully, as he returns*) You … you didn't see him, did you?

Georgina hastily sips her fresh drink

Georgina See *who*? I was at the pictures!
Henry When you were walking home. You didn't see a man running up and down the street in his underwear?
Georgina (*appalled*) No…!
Henry Apparently he's been going from door to door collecting money.
Georgina In his underwear?
Henry Yes.
Georgina W-what for?
Henry For the Boy Scouts.
Georgina Did … did *Rachel* give him anything?
Henry Oh, yes! *And* she gave him a glass of wine.
Georgina You mean this … this man in his … underwear was in here when you came in through the window?
Henry Yes! (*He laughs*) Rachel must have invited him in while she went to get her purse. Then gave him a glass of wine and sent him on to the next house.
Georgina (*relieved*) That's all right, then…

Henry finishes his drink, puts down the empty glass and starts to go

Henry Well, I think I'm going to have a hot bath. After all this excitement I'm feeling rather tired. (*He makes for the archway*)
Georgina Darling—?
Henry (*hesitating*) Yes?
Georgina You … you won't mention to Victor about tonight, will you?
Henry He probably knows about it already.
Georgina How?
Henry Well, this charity jogger will have called there by now, I expect. He'll be calling at all the houses. (*He laughs*) And to think, if our performance at the theatre hadn't been cancelled tonight I would have missed all this!

Henry goes out through the archway, laughing

Georgina looks ashen. She quickly finishes off her drink, collects his empty glass and is going into the kitchen as——

The Lights fade to Black-out

The Lights come up on Victor's and Rachel's house

*The front door bursts open and Rachel staggers in, casts her sports bag
aside and shuts the door, grateful for the sanctuary of her own home. In
need of a drink, she goes to get a whisky*

The doorbell rings

Puzzled, Rachel puts down her whisky and goes to open the front door

Frank, still in his underwear, falls into the room, gasping for breath

Frank I've been outside—hiding in a doorway—waiting for you!
Rachel You can't come in here!
Frank Well, I can't get on the bus dressed like this! Besides, I haven't any
money. (*Anxiously*) Your husband isn't at home, is he?
Rachel No. He's out. (*Puzzled*) Scottish dancing, apparently.
Frank This is all *your* fault!
Rachel Yes, I thought it would be…!
Frank You didn't have to go and tell everyone that I was jogging.
Rachel Well, I couldn't tell them what you were *really* up to, could I?
(*Suddenly realizing*) Why haven't you got your clothes back on?
Frank (*desperately*) Because they're upstairs at number thirty-five!
Rachel Well, go and get them!
Frank I can't! Your friend and her husband are there! *You*'ll have to lend me
some.
Rachel You're not getting on the bus in one of my dresses!
Frank (*seeing her sports bag*) What about your track-suit? I can borrow that.
(*He starts to go to the sports bag*)
Rachel (*suddenly remembering*) Oh, my God!
Frank What's the matter?
Rachel I haven't got it.
Frank Well, where is it?
Rachel It's under the sofa at number thirty-five!
Frank Well, you'll just have to lend me some of your husband's clothes.
Rachel I can't do that. He'd notice that they'd gone.
Frank (*desperately*) Well, say you've sent one of his suits to the cleaners!

Frank pushes Rachel out into the hall

*Frank starts to shake, nervously. He hastens to the front door, opens it a
fraction and peers out to see if the coast is clear. He shuts the door and tries
to stop shaking*

Rachel runs back in, carrying a suit of Victor's, and goes to Frank urgently

Rachel Here you are! I grabbed the first thing I could find. (*She thrusts the suit to him*)

Frank (*looking at it without enthusiasm*) Didn't you get a shirt?

Rachel Of course I didn't get a shirt!

Frank I can't wear a suit without a shirt...

Rachel Try getting on the bus dressed as you are, then!

Frank Oh, very well... (*He is about to put on the trousers*)

Whereupon, Victor walks in from the bathroom in a towelling bathrobe and sees Rachel in a sexy dress in the company of a strange man in his underwear

Victor What the hell's going on?

Frank quickly hides the suit behind his back. Rachel freezes in horror for a moment

Rachel We thought you were out.

Victor Well, I wasn't. I was having a bath. Until I heard you messing about in our bedroom.

Rachel You ... you decided not to go Scottish dancing, then?

Victor What are you talking about? Well? Is anyone going to tell me what this is all about?

Rachel Now, Victor—I know what you must be thinking——

Victor And you're right!

Rachel Well, you're wrong!

Victor I hope so!

Rachel There's a perfectly reasonable explanation. He was jogging.

Frank (*nervously, the suit behind his back*) Yes! You know— (*he demonstrates*) one, two! One, two! One, two!

Victor Yes. I know what jogging is. It's just that I didn't think people did it indoors.

Rachel He only stopped for a moment! To get his breath back!

Victor (*realizing*) Ah—you're the one who's been running up and down outside?

Frank Er ... yes. I'm afraid so.

Victor (*peering at him, suspiciously*) You some sort of exhibitionist?

Frank No! No, I—!

Rachel He's doing it for charity!

Victor Well, he could hardly charge for it, could he? (*He glowers at Frank*)

Rachel Sponsored jogging! He's going from house to house—collecting money—for the Boy Scouts!

Victor And that's why you came here? To collect money?

Frank Yes! That was the only reason!

Victor And has my wife given it to you?

Frank Er … yes…

Victor You'd better be on your way, then. You've a hell of a lot more houses to do yet. (*He moves away and sits on the sofa*)

Frank (*whispering to Rachel, urgently*) I shall need some money.

Rachel (*whispering also*) What?

Frank (*whispering*) For the bus!

Rachel (*whispering*) Oh. Yes. (*She gets some money from her sports bag and gives it to him, calling to Victor*) I'm giving him two pounds!

Victor (*uninterested*) Oh. Terrific.

Rachel (*to Frank, urgently*) Go on, then! (*She pushes Frank out of the front door*)

Frank disappears into the night, clutching the suit

Rachel closes the door, relieved, and moves down to Victor

Victor Did Henry find you all right? I told him you were at the rowing club.

Rachel Oh—yes.

Victor Bit of a surprise him turning up like that.

Rachel It certainly was…! (*Deliberately changing the subject*) And what were *you* up to tonight?

Victor (*nervously*) What?

Rachel Henry said you answered the door without your trousers on.

Victor I … I thought it was you—coming back early!

Rachel (*smiling, delightedly*) So you took your trousers off? You don't usually do that.

Victor I was going out!

Rachel Without your trousers? Oh, yes—of course! It was Scottish dancing, so you wouldn't need them.

Victor I was pressing them! Ready to go out. But I didn't.

Rachel Henry thought you had a woman in here…

Victor Don't be silly. Mrs Capstick doesn't clean on a Thursday evening.

Rachel I don't think he meant Mrs Capstick.

Victor (*wildly*) You shouldn't listen to Henry! He's an actor! His whole life is make-believe! (*He starts to go, anxious to avoid further questions*)

Rachel Where are you going?

Victor I—I thought I'd have an early night. I'm feeling rather tired. (*He turns in the doorway and looks back at her, suddenly puzzled*) Darling—?

Rachel Yes?

Victor Do you *always* dress like that when you're house-sitting?

Victor goes out into the hall

Rachel looks puzzled, wondering what on earth he was talking about. She collects her whisky, flops on to the sofa, and sips it, gratefully. Then she notices something... Slowly, she bends down to peer into the wastepaper basket. Intrigued, she reaches into it and brings out Georgina's evening bag...

The Lights come up on Georgina's and Henry's house

Henry, in a bathrobe, is coming in from upstairs, deep in thought. He is carrying Frank's shirt and trousers. He sits on the sofa, one item in each hand

Rachel looks at the handbag, deeply puzzled... Henry looks at the trousers and shirt, deeply puzzled... They both look up, thoughtfully, and turn in unison to call, inquiringly, in the direction of their respective unseen spouses

Henry ⎫ *(together)* Darling...?
Rachel ⎭

Black-out

ACT II

The same. About ten o'clock the following morning

The Lights come up on Victor's and Rachel's house. The wastepaper basket is now back in its original position

Mrs Capstick, the daily help, is below the sofa with the vacuum cleaner. A dreadful noise

Victor comes in from the bedrooms, wearing his towelling bathrobe. He is far from pleased and glares at Mrs Capstick

Victor Mrs Capstick… (*Then louder*) Mrs Capstick!

She hears him this time and turns to look at him

  (*Yelling*) Do you *have* to make that noise?
Mrs Capstick (*yelling back at him*) It's not me that's making the noise, it's the machine!
Victor (*yelling*) Well, turn it off!
Mrs Capstick (*yelling*) Won't pick up the dust if I turn it off!

Victor switches it off

A merciful peace. She stares at him, balefully

  What you want to go and do that for?
Victor I was having a lie-in. I can't lie-in with that racket going on.
Mrs Capstick Lie-in? It's ten o'clock on a Friday. Why aren't you at work? You're usually at work on a Friday. I've never seen you across my Hoover at ten o'clock on a Friday before.
Victor I'm taking the day off.
Mrs Capstick I see. A four-day week now, is it? I thought you were in advertising?
Victor I am.
Mrs Capstick Not much of an advertisement if you only work four days a week.

Victor I'll work a six-day week next week. (*He closes to her*) Now, look——

Mrs Capstick Don't you come near me dressed like that. I've read about people in the suburbs still without their clothes on at ten o'clock in the morning.

Victor I'll keep my distance.

Mrs Capstick Good.

Victor (*keeping his distance*) Look, Mrs Capstick—you do number thirty-five as well as us, don't you?

Mrs Capstick That's right. I do the two. Number thirty-five and number ten.

Victor Well, would you mind doing the other one first?

Mrs Capstick Number thirty-five before number ten?

Victor Yes, please.

Mrs Capstick Oh, I can't do that. I'm not yet due at number thirty-five. My ETA at number thirty-five is twelve noon.

Victor Well, just for once—switch us around!

Mrs Capstick (*doubtfully*) Switch you around?

Victor Thirty-five *now*! Ten at twelve!

Mrs Capstick Ten at twelve? Oh, no. I've got my routine to think of. You can't make free with my routine.

Victor (*wildly*) I'm not trying to make free with it. I just want you to alter it!

Mrs Capstick Don't you raise your voice to me. I'm not here to have people's voices raised.

Victor (*lowering his voice*) Why can't you co-operate?

Mrs Capstick I knew a woman once who was asked to co-operate by a man in a dressing-gown. She ended up having to resign from the bowls club.

Victor (*trying to be patient*) Look—you'll be doing me a favour.

Mrs Capstick That's what *he* told *her*!

Victor Please ... Mrs Capstick ... just this once. Go to number thirty-five now and return here at twelve noon.

Mrs Capstick I can't do that. Even if I wanted to I couldn't.

Victor Why not?

Mrs Capstick I'm employed by the *ladies* of number thirty-five and number ten. Not by the gentlemen. It's the ladies what pays my wages.

Victor sighs frustrated, and produces a five pound note from his dressing-gown pocket

Victor Here you are! I'll give you a bonus.

Mrs Capstick (*going to him, suspiciously*) Bonus?

Victor I'm offering you money!

Mrs Capstick That woman I told you about—*she* was offered money.

Victor There are no strings attached, Mrs Capstick. I know this probably sounds unlikely, but I am not seeking any favours from you in return for money.

Mrs Capstick Yes, you are. You're asking me to switch number thirty-five to ten and number ten to twelve. How much?

Victor What?

Mrs Capstick Bonus.

Victor Five? (*He holds out the note*)

Mrs Capstick No…!

Victor Ten? (*He holds out another note*)

Mrs Capstick Right.

Mrs Capstick grabs the money and goes quickly out of the front door

Rachel comes in from the kitchen

Rachel Where's Mrs Capstick?

Victor Oh, she … she just popped out.

Rachel I'm not paying her to pop out.

Victor She'll be back in a minute.

Rachel I hope so. She's left the Hoover in the walking way.

Victor I'll move it. (*He goes to move the vacuum cleaner*)

Rachel (*following him*) You don't have to do that.

Victor Why not?

Rachel You said she'll be back in a minute.

Victor Well … a couple of minutes. Maybe an hour. Hour and a half. (*He moves the cleaner out of the way*) Anyway, *I*'m going back to bed.

Rachel You're not *still* tired this morning, are you? You had a very early night. When I came upstairs you seemed to be fast asleep.

Victor (*vehemently*) Yes! I was! I was!

Rachel I expect you were exhausted after all your exertions.

Victor (*nervously*) W-what exertions?

Rachel Last night when I was out.

Victor If you were out how do you know about my exertions?

Rachel I put two and two together, of course.

Victor Which two twos was that?

Rachel You don't have to pretend.

Victor Well, I am *trying* to remember… Now, let me see… (*He tries to remember*) I had a small gin-and-tonic. Apart from that I had a fairly relaxed evening.

Rachel Victor—I know all about it!

Victor (*nervously*) What?!

Rachel I'm not an idiot. And, after all, you *are* a very attractive man.

Victor (*pleased*) Oh. Thank you very much. That's very nice of you. You don't usually tell me that. What have I done?

Rachel You don't expect me to go into the details, do you?
Victor W-which details are those?
Rachel The *grisly* details!
Victor Oh, dear. I didn't know there were any of those. How grisly?

Rachel goes to get the handbag from a drawer where she put it last night and places it on the sofa table, impressively. Victor stares at it in blank silence for a moment

What's this?
Rachel It's a handbag.
Victor Ah.
Rachel A *lady*'s handbag. A lady's *evening* handbag.
Victor (*astonished*) Is it really? Good Lord.
Rachel And it doesn't belong to *me*.
Victor Well, it doesn't belong to me!
Rachel Then what is it doing in our house?
Victor Is that where it was?
Rachel Yes. And there isn't another woman living here, is there?
Victor (*thinking deeply*) Well, I only entered *one* woman on the electoral roll...
Rachel So presumably it must belong to some other woman! Victor! You had somebody here last night, didn't you?
Victor D-did I? (*He escapes from her below the sofa*)
Rachel No wonder you had your trousers off when Henry called. Who was she?
Victor I don't know what you're talking about. I was alone last night. Except when Henry called.
Rachel I expect you got her out of the way—and in her hurry she left her handbag behind. Is that what happened?
Victor (*apparently outraged*) I'm surprised at you, Rachel. I really am. Surprised and hurt. You don't really think that I—of *all* people—would invite another woman in when you were out?
Rachel Well, that's what it looks like. How else would a lady's handbag get here? And you know where it was? In the wastepaper basket! How's that for kinky?

Victor stares at her for a moment, apparently realizing something

Victor In the wastepaper basket?
Rachel Yes.
Victor (*going to it*) *This* wastepaper basket?
Rachel Yes.

Victor (*smiling, suddenly relaxed*) Oh, it's *that* handbag!
Rachel What?
Victor I didn't know it was that one.
Rachel (*following him*) So you *knew* there was a handbag?
Victor Of course I knew! (*A beat*) Mrs Capstick left it there.
Rachel *Our* Mrs Capstick?
Victor Yes.
Rachel The one who was—?
Victor Hoovering. Yes.
Rachel (*laughing*) Don't be silly, darling. Why should Mrs Capstick put her
   handbag in the wastepaper basket?
Victor (*with overwhelming logic*) Because she'd *finished* with it! (*He
   escapes below the sofa*)
Rachel Finished with it?
Victor Yes. She told me all about it this morning. She said, "I'm fed up with
   my old handbag, Mr Parker. I've had it a long time and I'm getting bored
   with it. So I've thrown it into the wastepaper basket."

Rachel considers this for a moment

Rachel She said that this morning?
Victor Yes.
Rachel But it was in the wastepaper basket last night.
Victor (*on the back foot*) Sorry?
Rachel I saw it there *last night*.

A beat

Victor Ah. Yes. So did I. That's the first time *I* saw it, too. But she put it there
   last week! I'm surprised neither of us saw it before, but we're such busy
   people, aren't we? Always racing about. I know I am. Never a spare
   moment. Certainly no time to go crawling about looking in wastepaper
   baskets for discarded handbags.
Rachel You don't really expect me to believe all this, do you?
Victor (*innocently*) Why not?
Rachel Mrs Capstick would never have a handbag like *that*! It's far too
   glamorous for her.
Victor I don't see why. She's probably very glamorous underneath all that.
Rachel She'd have something more ... more practical.
Victor (*with sudden inspiration*) Ah—*I* know.
Rachel Do you?
Victor Yes. I hope so. She probably got *this* handbag for when she goes out
   dancing.

Rachel (*puzzled*) Dancing?

Victor Ballroom dancing. You can't go ballroom dancing with any rotten old handbag.

Rachel I didn't know Mrs Capstick went ballroom dancing.

Victor Good Lord, yes! She's won awards for her tango. I'm surprised she hasn't told you about it.

Rachel No. She's never mentioned it…

Victor Ah—that's because she's modest. She only told *me* in the strictest confidence. So … it would be best if you … if you didn't mention it to her. We don't want to embarrass her, do we? It might put her off her Hoovering. (*He sighs, happily, and wanders away, thinking he has covered his tracks*) So … so that's all right, then, isn't it?

Rachel What is?

Victor Well—about the handbag. Now you know how it came to be … where it was. (*He smiles at her, hopefully*)

Rachel Oh, darling…! (*She approaches him at speed*)

Victor (*alarmed for a moment*) What?

Rachel (*embracing him*) I'm sorry. I shouldn't have been so suspicious. Fancy me thinking you had a lover.

Victor is not sure that this is very flattering

Victor Sorry?

Rachel Well, it's ridiculous, isn't it?

Victor Is it?

Rachel Of course it is.

Victor I thought you said just now that I was a very attractive man?

Rachel But you're not like that, are you? I'm sorry, darling. I should have trusted you.

Victor Of course you should.

Rachel I will in future. (*She kisses him and goes towards the front door*)

Victor (*quietly*) Thank God for that…! You off shopping?

Rachel I'm going to have coffee with Georgina.

Victor (*alert, like a bird*) At number thirty-five?

Rachel Well, that's where she lives.

Victor *Now?*

Rachel (*amused*) I don't think she's moved since yesterday.

Victor I mean you're going *now*?

Rachel You don't mind, do you? You said you were going back to bed. I shan't be long. (*She smiles, warmly*) I'm sorry I suspected you.

Victor That's all right.

Rachel I'm sure you're just as faithful to me as I am to you.

Rachel goes

Victor is unsure about her last words. He races across to pick up the mobile telephone and starts to tap, frantically, as he goes out to the bedroom

The Lights fade to Black-out

The Lights come up on Henry's and Georgina's house

Mrs Capstick is below the sofa with the vacuum cleaner. A dreadful noise

Henry comes in from the bedroom, wearing a colourful silk dressing-gown and carrying a mobile phone. He is far from pleased and glares at Mrs Capstick

Henry Mrs Capstick... (*Then louder*) Mrs Capstick! (*Impatiently, he switches off the cleaner at the socket*)

Mrs Capstick jumps with fright. She turns and sees him

Mrs Capstick Oh, my God! Not another one!
Henry What?
Mrs Capstick Another man in his dressing-gown.
Henry You're not usually here at this time.
Mrs Capstick Well, there's been a change of plan. I'm doing you now and number ten at twelve. (*She switches the cleaner on again*)

Henry hastily switches it off again

Henry That isn't what we arranged! I'm in bed now. You can't be here when I'm in bed.
Mrs Capstick Oh. Another one having a lie-in, eh?
Henry What?
Mrs Capstick The men around here seem to spend half their lives in bed.
Henry I'm an actor! I work in the theatre at night! Entertaining my public! So I think I'm entitled to a lie-in in the morning. You're supposed to be here at noon. Not now.
Mrs Capstick And that gives you time to get your clothes on, does it, luvvie?
Henry (*glaring at her*) This is for you! (*He holds out the mobile*)
Mrs Capstick (*moved*) Oh, you didn't have to buy me a present.
Henry (*trying to be patient*) The mobile is mine; the *call* is for you. (*He thrusts it at her again*)
Mrs Capstick A call? For me?
Henry Yes! (*He thrusts it into her hands*)
Mrs Capstick I don't usually get calls when I'm doing for one of my ladies.

Henry I should answer it if I were you. You've probably won the bloody lottery!

Henry takes the vacuum cleaner out into the kitchen

Mrs Capstick speaks into the mobile, nervously

Mrs Capstick Hullo? Yes, Mrs Capstick speaking... (*Disappointed*) Oh, it's you. Thought you'd be asleep by now. (*Not too pleased*) What? Number ten now and number thirty-five at twelve... I see. Right.

Henry returns

She thrusts the mobile back at him

There's been another change of plan. I'm doing number ten now and number thirty-five at twelve.
Henry Oh, splendid! That *is* good news. Thank you, Mrs Capstick.

Henry embraces the astonished Mrs Capstick and goes back upstairs

Mrs Capstick (*calling after him*) I'll be back at high noon, so make sure you've got your clothes on by then! (*She goes to open the front door*)

Rachel has just arrived outside

All right, all right! I'm coming! You don't have to chase me!

She lets the bewildered Rachel in

Rachel Is Mrs Brent in?
Mrs Capstick No. She's down the supermarket. And he's upstairs in bed. (*She starts to go*)
Rachel Mrs Capstick——
Mrs Capstick (*hesitating*) Yes?
Rachel At least now we know what to buy you for Christmas.
Mrs Capstick Sorry?
Rachel (*with a big smile*) A new handbag!

Totally bewildered, Mrs Capstick disappears, closing the door behind her

Rachel looks, anxiously, in the direction of the bedrooms and then goes, quickly, across to the sofa. She bends down and tries to retrieve her track-suit from underneath it. She cannot reach it. Desperately, she goes on to her hands and knees and tries again. Still no success. She runs to the front door, grabs a walking-stick and returns to resume her position on all fours, and tries to pull the track-suit out by using the walking-stick as a rake

Whereupon, Henry walks in from upstairs and sees her

Henry Rachel!

Rachel sees him and freezes, clutching the walking-stick

Rachel I … I thought you were asleep.
Henry I was trying to be! What the hell are you doing down there?

Rachel tries to think what she was doing down there

Rachel I … I'm looking for an ear-ring.
Henry With a walking-stick?
Rachel I lost one last night. So I was looking for it. (*She looks for it*)
Henry Don't tell me you were wearing ear-rings while you were rowing?
Rachel When I got back! I put them on when I got back.
Henry After you'd put on one of Georgina's dresses?
Rachel (*getting up from the floor*) Yes—exactly. Somehow that dress needed ear-rings.
Henry Which you happened to have with you?
Rachel Ah—no—no, the ear-rings belonged to Georgina.
Henry So you borrowed Georgina's dress—*and* her ear-rings?
Rachel Yes! (*She runs away to put the walking-stick back where it belongs*)
Henry What about shoes? Did you borrow shoes as well?
Rachel Er … yes.
Henry You seem to have been going through her entire wardrobe! So you borrowed her ear-rings and then lost one?
Rachel Yes. It … it must have come off.
Henry How? Were you engaged in mortal combat? Or were you just over-excited by seeing the charity jogger in his underwear?

Rachel returns to him, trying to laugh it off

Rachel Don't be silly, Henry! What has the charity jogger to do with it?
Henry I'm beginning to wonder…! Better help yourself to coffee. Georgina shouldn't be long. (*He starts to go, then hesitates*) By the way, I found your wet clothes.
Rachel Sorry?

Henry The ones you took off after you fell in the river.

Rachel You ... you *found* them?

Henry Yes. Upstairs.

Rachel (*blankly*) Sorry?

Henry A pair of denims and a shirt. Bit on the large side for you, I'd have thought. But I showed them to Georgina last night and she said they belonged to you.

Rachel *Georgina* said that?

Henry Yes.

Rachel Ah—then they *do*!

Henry They'd dried off quite well, actually. Had you given them a whirl in the tumble-dryer?

Rachel Er ... just a brief whirl, yes.

Henry Then left them in a bundle on the bed?

Rachel Well, I ... I was in a hurry.

Henry Yes, I bet you were. The only thing that puzzles me is why you were wearing trousers and a shirt while you were rowing. No wonder you fell in the river!

Henry grins and disappears upstairs

Rachel, in despair, runs out into the kitchen as——

The Lights fade to Black-out

The Lights come up on Victor's and Rachel's house. The doorbell is ringing

Victor comes in from the bedroom. He is now dressed in casual clothes. He opens the door

Mrs Capstick marches in, angrily

Mrs Capstick I wish you'd make up your mind!

Victor Yes—I'm sorry about that, but something unexpected turned up.

Mrs Capstick Well, at least you've got your trousers on. That's something. I'm not one to be messed about by men without trousers.

Victor No, I know you're not!

Mrs Capstick So I take it we're back to square one—number ten now, number thirty-five at twelve?

Victor Yes, that's right.

Mrs Capstick Does this mean that I have to return my bonus?

Victor Oh, no—of course not!

Mrs Capstick That's all right, then. I'll get on. (*She heads for the vacuum cleaner*)

Victor Mrs Capstick——
Mrs Capstick (*hesitating*) Yes?
Victor (*with a warm smile*) There's ... there's no hurry, is there?
Mrs Capstick Sorry?
Victor You don't have to rush into it.
Mrs Capstick (*suspiciously*) Hullo—what's this?
Victor Why don't you sit down for a minute? (*He sits on the sofa*)
Mrs Capstick What you getting at?
Victor I'm not getting at anything, Mrs Capstick. I just thought you might
    like to sit down and ... and have a little chat. (*He pats the sofa,
    encouragingly*)
Mrs Capstick A chat? With *you*?
Victor Why not?
Mrs Capstick I don't usually chat with my ladies' gentlemen. It's not on my
    agenda.
Victor You can make an exception, can't you? In *my* case? (*He indicates the
    place next to him*) Please...

*Slowly, her eyes glued to him, Mrs Capstick sits carefully next to him, keeping
her distance*

Mrs Capstick What's this all about?
Victor I want you to do me a favour.
Mrs Capstick (*standing up at once*) Oh, no! I'm not having none of that! Just
    'cos you've paid me a bonus doesn't give you the freedom of the city.
Victor No, no—it's nothing like that!
Mrs Capstick You sure?
Victor Positive...!
Mrs Capstick That's all right, then. (*She resumes her seat, keeping a wary
    eye on him*)

*Victor picks up the handbag and holds it out to her. She stares at it,
uncomprehendingly*

    What's this?
Victor It's your handbag.
Mrs Capstick Sorry?
Victor This handbag belongs to you.
Mrs Capstick But it's not Christmas *yet*!
Victor (*puzzled*) Sorry?
Mrs Capstick You giving me this?
Victor No!
Mrs Capstick You're *not* giving me this?

Victor Not officially, no.

Mrs Capstick (*suspicious again*) You mean you don't want your *wife* to know! I'm off! (*She gets up again*)

Victor No, Mrs Capstick! You misunderstand!

Mrs Capstick If a gentleman gives a lady a gift without his wife knowing about it there's only one thing on *his* agenda! (*She starts to go*)

Victor No, no!

Mrs Capstick (*hesitating*) No?

Victor Please sit down...

Mrs Capstick (*relenting*) You've got a way with you, Mr Parker, I'll say that for you. (*She sits down again*)

Victor Now, the thing is—my wife found this handbag here last night, and it doesn't belong to *her*, so... (*He leaves the sentence in the air*)

Mrs Capstick So she thought it belonged to "someone else"? (*With a world-weary sigh*) I understand...

Victor (*surprised*) You *do*?

Mrs Capstick Oh, yes. I do read the Sunday papers, you know. So your wife thinks you've been up to no good while she was out of the way?

Victor Well, you're a man of the world, Mrs Capstick. You know what women are like. They see things and they put two and two together.

Mrs Capstick And where do I fit into this scenario?

Victor I told my wife that this handbag belonged to you.

Mrs Capstick Oh, I see. So this is all a question of pretence?

Victor Exactly.

Mrs Capstick To *your* advantage, I assume?

Victor Well ... yes.

Mrs Capstick considers the situation

Mrs Capstick I don't suppose this question of pretence involves an additional bonus, by any chance?

Patiently, Victor produces another note

Right! (*She takes the money, gets up and starts to go, carrying the handbag*)

Victor leaps up and races around to catch her

Victor You can't take the handbag!

Mrs Capstick I thought it was mine.

Victor No, no. That's the pretence. The *real* owner will want it back. (*He takes it back*)

Mrs Capstick (*doubtfully*) Oh, I don't know about that.

Victor passes her another note

   Right! I'll carry on in the bedroom.

Mrs Capstick picks up the cleaner and goes, quickly

   Victor smiles with relief, hastily puts the handbag into a plastic bag from the chest of drawers and is going into the kitchen as the Lights fade to Black-out

The Lights come up on Georgina's and Henry's house

   The front door opens and Frank comes in, cautiously. He is wearing Victor's suit (with no shirt) which is too small (or too large) for him. He moves down into the room, looking about, nervously

   Rachel walks in from the kitchen with a cup of coffee, sees the back of an apparent stranger and gasps

Rachel Ah!
Frank Ah! (*He turns in surprise*)
Rachel Frank! What are *you* doing here?
Frank I've come to get my clothes.
Rachel (*whispering, urgently*) You can't! Georgina's husband is upstairs!
Frank What?!
Rachel S'sh!
Frank Why isn't he at work?
Rachel He's an actor! And actors are like bats. They only appear during the hours of darkness.
Frank Oh, my God…!
Rachel How did you get in?
Frank The spare key from under the garden gnome.
Rachel You mean you put it back there after you got in last night?
Frank Of course! That's what I usually do. What are *you* doing here, anyway?
Rachel I came to get my track-suit. But I can't find it!
Frank Oh, no…! (*He wanders away in a high state of agitation*)

Rachel becomes aware of his ill-fitting suit and starts to laugh

   What are you laughing at?

Rachel Well, it's not a very good fit, is it? (*She giggles some more*)

Frank Of course it's not a very good fit! It's not mine, is it?

Rachel (*going to him*) Why are you still wearing it? I only lent you Victor's suit to go home in.

Frank I couldn't get into my flat!

Rachel Why not?

Frank Because my key's in my trousers, and my trousers are upstairs!

Rachel So where did you spend the night?

Frank In a bus shelter.

Rachel laughs

It's not funny! I was thrown out twice by the police.

Rachel So you came back to get your key as well as your clothes?

Frank Of course I did! I couldn't go to work dressed like this, could I?

Rachel And didn't you get any breakfast?

Frank No. I stopped at a workmen's café with the change out of the two pounds you gave me, but they didn't want to serve me. They thought I was a tramp.

Rachel Oh, Frank, you poor thing…!

Frank (*desperately*) How the hell am I going to get my clothes and my key if Georgina's husband is upstairs? *He* mustn't see them!

Rachel It's too late. He already has.

Frank What?!

Rachel He found them last night.

Frank (*appalled*) Oh, my God…!

Rachel There's worse to come. Georgina told him they belonged to *me*!

Frank To *you*?

Rachel Yes!

Frank (*cheering up*) Oh, well, that's all right, then, isn't it? He won't suspect *me*.

Rachel It may be all right for you, but it's not all right for me. Henry thinks I was rowing down the river dressed as a man!

The front door opens, and Georgina comes in with various shopping bags and a tweed jacket from the cleaners. She pushes the door shut behind her and walks out into the kitchen without apparently having seen Rachel and Frank. A loud crash in the kitchen as she reacts and drops the shopping. She runs back in and stares at Rachel

Georgina Rachel! What are *you* doing here?

Rachel Having coffee. Is that all right?

Georgina looks at Frank, inquiringly

Oh, this is Frank.

Georgina Ah! So *you*'re Frank! (*Amused*) I hear you've been jogging for charity.

Frank It was her idea!

Rachel Well, you were in your underwear. I had to say *some*thing.

Georgina You poor things! Henry was supposed to be at the theatre. It must have been a terrible shock for you.

Frank Yes, it was…!

Georgina But why are you both here *now*? You can't start all over again this morning! Henry's here!

Rachel Yes, I know!

Frank I came to get my clothes.

Georgina I *wondered* why you were wearing that suit!

Rachel It's one of Victor's.

Georgina (*laughing*) It's not a very good fit…!

Frank It was an emergency!

Rachel Why on earth did you tell Henry that Frank's clothes belonged to me?

Georgina How else could I explain a man's clothes in our spare bedroom?

Rachel You don't think Henry suspects, do you? About me and Frank?

Georgina He'd better not!

Rachel No. Because if he does he might tell Victor!

Frank (*alarmed*) He wouldn't do that, would he?

Georgina He might. You know what men are like. They talk.

Frank Then I'd better go! (*He starts to go*)

Rachel You can't go yet. You haven't got your key and clothes. (*To Georgina*) Where did you put them?

Georgina In the kitchen.

Rachel (*to Frank*) So go and change.

Frank I can't change in the kitchen!

Georgina Well, what do you *want* to do? Go upstairs and face my husband?

Frank I'll change in the kitchen.

Frank hastens out into the kitchen

Rachel sits down on the sofa with her coffee

Rachel I'm not sure Victor would mind, anyway.

Georgina Mind about what?

Rachel About me and Frank.

Georgina Of course he would!

Rachel Well, he was behaving in a very strange way this morning.

Georgina Was he?

Rachel *Very* strange.

Georgina In what way?

Rachel Furtive.
Georgina Strange and furtive?
Rachel Yes.
Georgina Surely not? Victor's not a furtive sort of person.
Rachel Apparently last night he told Henry that he was going Scottish
    dancing.
Georgina (*astonished*) Victor?
Rachel Yes. He's never been Scottish dancing in his life. If you ask me I think
    he was covering something up.
Georgina W-what sort of thing?
Rachel Last night I found a lady's handbag in our wastepaper basket.
Georgina What?!
Rachel I *thought* you'd be surprised.
Georgina A—a—a lady's handbag?
Rachel Yes! So naturally I was suspicious.
Georgina Naturally!
Rachel I thought at first that he must have had a woman in there.
Georgina (*over-doing her reaction*) Victor?!
Rachel Well, it wasn't *my* handbag.
Georgina Er ... whose handbag was it, then?
Rachel You'll never guess!
Georgina W-won't I?
Rachel Mrs Capstick's!
Georgina (*surprised*) *Our* Mrs Capstick?
Rachel Yes.
Georgina The one who does the—?
Rachel Hoovering. Yes.

They both laugh

Georgina (*relieved*) Oh, well, that's all right, then, isn't it? He's hardly likely
    to be having an affair with her, is he? So you needn't be suspicious any
    more. Victor wouldn't do a thing like that.
Rachel He'd better not!

Henry comes in from upstairs. He is now dressed

*Rachel and Georgina exchange a look, both anxious about who is in the
kitchen*

Henry Still here, then, Rachel?
Georgina Henry! I thought you were having a lie-in.
Henry I was. But it's not very easy with all this gossiping going on down
    here. (*To Rachel*) Did you *find* what you were looking for?

Rachel Er ... no.

Henry (*to Georgina*) I'm afraid Rachel's lost one of your ear-rings, darling.

Georgina (*puzzled*) Sorry?

Henry Didn't she tell you? Last night she borrowed a pair of your ear-rings to go with your dress and shoes, and she mislaid one. We'd better all have a good look. (*He goes on to his hands and knees and searches, desperately, lifting Rachel's legs abruptly out of the way*)

Georgina Henry, don't be silly! Henry! It doesn't matter about the ear-ring. (*She pulls him to his feet*)

Henry Doesn't it?

Georgina No. Of course not.

Rachel I probably dropped it when I got back home.

Henry Oh. Well, Mrs Capstick will have Hoovered it up by now. You brought the dress back, I presume?

Georgina Darling, don't be so rude.

Henry I was only asking if she brought your dress back.

Rachel I ... I'll fetch it later.

Henry And the shoes, don't forget! (*He remembers something*) Ah! Now—talking about shoes... (*He goes to get Frank's trainers out of a drawer and brings them to Rachel, triumphantly*) There you are.

Rachel and Georgina stare at the trainers in surprise

Go on—take them!

Rachel Sorry?

Henry Well, they are *yours*, aren't they?

Rachel Mine?

Henry I found them upstairs with your other things last night. The things you got wet when you fell in the river. (*To Georgina*) You remember, darling? You told me they belonged to Rachel, didn't you?

Georgina I remember the trousers and shirt. I don't remember there being any shoes...

Henry Of course there were shoes! She couldn't wander about the boathouse in bare feet, could she? So there you are! (*He thrusts the trainers at Rachel*)

Rachel stares at the shoes, bleakly

What's the matter? Don't you think they'll fit?

Rachel Well, I...

Henry You'd better try them on. (*He kneels down beside her*) Come on! Foot up!

Reluctantly, Rachel raises her foot. Henry holds it and removes her shoe. He glances up at Georgina with a big smile

Like a scene out of Cinderella, isn't it? (*He puts one of the trainers on to Rachel's foot. It is, of course, much too big*)

Rachel sits there, deeply embarrassed

Oh. Oh, dear. It doesn't seem to fit very well, does it? (*Deeply puzzled*) I can't understand that, can you? You'd expect that after getting soaked in the river, they'd have shrunk, not stretched... (*He takes the offending shoe off, gets up and puts the pair of trainers down on the sofa table*) I should take them back to the shop and complain, if I were you. (*He goes towards the kitchen*)

Georgina Where are you going?
Henry Into the kitchen.

Rachel and Georgina panic

Rachel ⎫ (*together*) No!!
Georgina ⎭
Henry What?
Georgina You—you can't go in there!
Henry Why not? I *live* here.
Georgina Yes, but——
Henry I was only going to make a cup of coffee.
Georgina There isn't any!
Henry No coffee?
Georgina No.
Henry (*indicating Rachel's cup*) She's got some.
Rachel This was the last!
Georgina Yes! And now we've run out!
Henry But you've just been shopping. Don't tell me Sainsbury's have run out of coffee? Never mind. I'll have tea. (*He starts to go again*)
Georgina There isn't any water!
Henry Sorry?
Georgina There's been a water shortage lately. You must have read about it. It's been in all the papers.
Henry (*puzzled*) Has it?
Georgina Yes, of course! And it was on the radio this morning. They think there's going to be a drought. So they've turned the water off as a precaution.
Henry Well, I expect there'll be enough still in the kettle for one cup of tea. (*He tries to go again*)
Rachel No! I used the last drop just now.
Henry Well, I think that was very inconsiderate. You don't even live here. (*To Georgina*) Didn't they give us any warning?

Georgina Sorry?

Henry About turning the water off. We could have filled a few saucepans. That's what you're supposed to do. Have they erected a standpipe in the road? I could go and get a bucketful.

Georgina No. I don't think so...

Henry What a pity. And I really fancied a cup of coffee. (*Suddenly*) Ah! *I know!*

Georgina What?

Henry (*to Rachel*) I'll go along to *your* house. I'm sure Victor will have had the sense to fill a jug of water.

Henry hastens, optimistically, out of the front door

Georgina and Rachel exchange a frantic look. Georgina goes quickly towards the kitchen

Georgina (*calling as she goes*) Frank!

Georgina disappears into the kitchen and returns almost immediately

He's not there! He must have gone out of the back door.

Rachel Thank God for that! Come on! We'd better get Victor's suit out of the way before Henry comes back!

Rachel and Georgina race out into the kitchen as——

The Lights fade to Black-out

The Lights come up on Victor's and Rachel's house. Someone is outside, ringing the doorbell

Victor comes in from the kitchen with a mug of coffee. He opens the front door

Henry is there

Henry May I come in?

Victor Of course.

Henry walks into the room, grimly. Victor closes the front door and follows him, puzzled

Is something wrong?

Henry There certainly is! I'm afraid there's a bit of a crisis.

Victor W-what sort of crisis?

Henry Georgina's just told me all about it.

Victor (*guiltily*) *Told* you?!

Henry That's why I'm here.

Victor W-why? It … it's nothing to do with *me*, is it?

Henry Of course it's to do with you! *You* won't be able to escape. We live in the same street.

Victor Oh, my God! What did she tell you exactly?

Henry notices Victor's coffee with surprise

Henry Ah! I see you've *got* one!

Victor (*puzzled*) Sorry?

Henry Coffee! You've got a cup of coffee.

Victor Is that unusual? Anyway, by the sound of it I'll need more than a cup of coffee…

Henry What are you talking about?

Victor I hope violence is ruled out?

Henry Depends how soon they get a standpipe in the road.

Victor How did it all come out?

Henry It *didn't* come out, that's the trouble!

Victor If it didn't come out, how do you know?

Henry Because Georgina *told* me!

Victor I can't think why she even mentioned it…!

Henry There didn't seem any point in keeping it a secret. I'd have been bound to find out sooner or later.

Victor And that's why you came to see *me*?

Henry Of course! I came here as soon as I heard about it.

Victor Well, that's only natural, I suppose… How did Rachel take it?

Henry (*puzzled*) Naturally, she's just as upset as everyone else.

Victor Yes, I suppose she would be. Poor kid, finding out like that…

Henry But *she*'d already *had* hers.

Victor Sorry?

Henry She'd already finished with hers.

Victor Finished? I didn't know she'd started! I didn't know anything about it.

Henry Neither did I! It came as a surprise to me, I can tell you. You don't expect this sort of thing in a civilised suburb.

Victor No. No, and I … and I'm sorry. I would have understood if you'd hit me.

Henry Hit you? Of course I didn't hit you! We can't have civil disobedience about a thing like this. I mean, it's not all that serious, is it?

Victor No—of course it isn't—!

Henry (*laughing*) It's not the end of the world.

Victor Well, it's very good of you to take it like this. And I do appreciate it.

Henry I'm surprised Mrs Capstick didn't know about it.

Victor Thank God she didn't! It would have been public knowledge by now.

Henry Apparently, it already is.

Victor What?!

Henry Georgina said it was on the radio this morning.

Victor How the hell did *they* get to hear about it?

Henry Well, it's their job to find out, isn't it? About things like this.

Victor (*sombrely*) Henry, I'm glad you're being so civilised and understanding about it.

Henry Sorry?

Victor The important thing now is for us to start building bridges…

Henry No need for bridges if the river's dried up!

Victor That's very philosophical. (*Regretfully*) But it should never have happened, of course…

Henry It wouldn't have done if the bloody council had been more on the ball! I shall write a letter to them.

Victor No, no—there's no need for that. I don't think we want the council involved.

Henry It's their responsibility!

Victor Is it?

Henry It's in the local by-laws!

Victor Good Lord…!

Henry Anyway, did you manage to fill a couple of buckets?

Victor stares at him, blankly, at a total loss

Victor Sorry?

Henry (*smiling, knowingly*) Ah! I knew it! You were wise before the event and filled the bath, didn't you?

Victor (*puzzled*) Filled the bath? No…

Henry Don't say you didn't even fill the bloody kettle?

Victor What?

Henry Before they turned it off!

Victor What are you talking about?

Henry They've turned the water off! That's what I've been telling you.

Victor Who have?

Henry Whoever's in charge of it! The Water Board. They've turned it off. We've no bloody water! I came here to see if *you* could spare me a drop so I could have a cup of coffee!

Victor takes a long time to digest this. Finally, he realizes that he must try to carry off the dreadful misunderstanding. He laughs, nervously

Victor (*enthusiastically*) Of course! I'll get you a cup of coffee right away! (*He hastens to the kitchen doorway*) Digestive biscuit? Piece of cake?

Victor darts out into the kitchen

Henry chuckles, happily, for a moment, then begins to wonder what they have been talking about

Henry Victor…?

Henry goes into the kitchen, puzzled, as the Lights fade to Black-out

The Lights come up in Georgina and Henry's house. Someone is outside, knocking on the front door

Georgina and Rachel come in from the kitchen

Rachel remains near the kitchen door. Georgina goes to open the front door

Procter is there, his unseen dog pulling at the leash and barking

Georgina What the hell do *you* want?
Procter I caught a man climbing over your garden wall!

He produces Frank and thrusts him into the room. Frank is now wearing his own clothes, but still in his stockinged feet

(*To his dog*) Now sit. Sit…! Good boy. (*He casts the leash aside and comes into the house*)
Frank (*to Georgina*) Has your husband gone?
Georgina Yes. He's down the road with Victor.
Frank Thank God for that…!

Having closed the front door, Procter arrives and jabs a finger towards Frank

Procter I've been watching him. That's what we do in Neighbourhood Watch. We watch people.
Georgina Yes. I suppose you would…
Procter Especially people like him. Furtive people!
Frank Look, I can explain—!
Procter This sort of thing is food and drink to me, sonny. I've looked into the eyes of enough criminals to know one when I see one.

Frank I'm not a criminal!

Procter Then why were you climbing over the garden wall in your socks?

Rachel I'm sure there's a perfectly simple explanation.

Frank (*seeing his trainers*) Ah! There they are! (*He sits in the armchair and puts them on, relieved*)

Procter (*seeing Rachel*) Mrs Parker! So *you*'re back again?

Georgina (*to Rachel*) Have you two met before, then?

Rachel Last night!

Georgina (*amused*) Oh, no...!

Procter You were lucky he didn't take advantage of you.

Rachel Yes, I suppose I was... (*She exchanges an amused smile with Georgina*)

Procter (*going to glare at Frank*) I was suspicious of you the moment I set eyes on you.

Frank Yes, I know you were...

Procter (*to Rachel*) I fear you have been taken in by a common con-man.

Frank I'm not that!

Procter *I* know what happened here last night... (*He casts a severe glance at Frank*)

Rachel (*quietly, to Georgina*) *I* know what *didn't* happen here last night...!

Procter He lulled you into a false sense of security by cooking you those little... (*with distaste*) "bits and pieces". And all the time he was waiting his moment to pounce!

Rachel *Were* you, Frank? I didn't know that...

Rachel and Georgina giggle

Procter Jogging was only a cover for his deeper purpose.

Frank What deeper purpose?

Procter Helping himself to other people's property!

Frank *What?*

Procter I saw you entering number ten and leaving later carrying a suit. A suit that you had presumably stolen from this lady's husband!

Frank I only borrowed it...

Procter You then proceeded to lurk in a doorway in a suspicious manner while you donned the stolen suit! Constable Weaver will be very interested in people who lurk in doorways in broad daylight to put their clothes on.

Frank It's better than lurking in doorways and taking them off!

Procter And no doubt the other intruder at number ten was your accomplice?

Rachel What other intruder?

Procter I spotted a lady leaving through an open window.

Rachel At number ten?

Procter Yes. Climbing down a drainpipe and running away.

Georgina (*nervously*) D-did you get a good look at her?

Procter No. She was going too fast for me.

Georgina (*quietly*) Thank God for that…!

Rachel You must have been mistaken.

Georgina Of course he was mistaken! Mr Procter, your imagination is running away with you.

Procter It was the woman who was running away!

Rachel But Victor was in all the evening. He'd have known if anyone had been there. Wouldn't he, Georgina?

Georgina He certainly would! And there wasn't!

Procter (*taking out his mobile*) Nevertheless, I'd better report to Constable Weaver that I have apprehended a potential villain… (*He starts to punch in figures*)

Frank leaps up and goes, urgently, to Procter

Frank But I can explain!

Procter Leaving this house by way of the garden wall? You can explain that, can you?

Frank I … I was visiting.

Procter Visiting? I've never known a visitor of *mine* to leave through the back garden.

Rachel Mr Procter! You're misunderstanding the situation! This young man is a friend of us both. Isn't he, Georgina?

Georgina Yes. (*Quietly to Rachel*) More friendly with one than with the other…

Rachel gives her a look

Procter (*finding it hard to believe*) Are you telling me that you aren't in any danger from this intruder?

Rachel Of course we're not!

Reluctantly, Procter puts away his mobile and prepares to leave

Procter In that case I shall have to take my dog elsewhere in our pursuit of crime. (*He turns at the front door and glares at Frank*) But I'll still be keeping an eye on *you*!

Procter goes. Outside, his dog barks noisily as they disappear down the road

Georgina (*to Frank*) You'd better go before Henry comes back!

Frank (*plaintively*) Couldn't I have some food first? I never had any breakfast!

Georgina and Rachel laugh

Georgina Oh, all right.

Georgina and Rachel are taking Frank into the kitchen as the Lights fade to Black-out

The Lights come up on Rachel's and Victor's house

Henry comes in from the kitchen with a mug of coffee

He sits on the sofa, thoughtfully, and sips his coffee

Victor follows him in, apprehensively, holding out a biscuit tin

Victor Are you *sure* you wouldn't like a biscuit?
Henry Quite sure, thank you.
Victor We've got quite a selection. (*Examining the contents of the tin*) Chocolate digestive, custard cream, thin arrowroot…
Henry I don't want a biscuit!
Victor No. Right. (*He puts the biscuit tin down*)

Henry sips his coffee

Did I put enough sugar in?
Henry The coffee's fine!
Victor Oh. Good. (*He pauses*) Something's worrying you, though, isn't it?
Henry Yes! It *is*!
Victor I could tell. (*He sits beside him, nervously*) I… I suppose you want to talk about it?
Henry I certainly do! Why the hell should they turn the water off in *my* house and not *yours*?
Victor (*relieved*) Oh … ah … er—well, we must be on a … on a different circuit.
Henry Circuit? We're talking water not electricity.
Victor Isn't it the same sort of system?
Henry Hardly. You'd find it pretty difficult sending water along a wire.
Victor Yes. I suppose so…

A pause

Henry It's pipes, you know.

Victor Sorry?

Henry For the water. They use pipes.

Victor Ah—yes.

Henry (*profoundly*) I imagine they have one big pipe. Running the whole length of this street. With lesser pipes ... leading from the big pipe ... into each of our houses.

Victor Sounds sensible.

Henry And yet they managed to cut *us* off and not *you*.

Victor (*with a shrug*) That's modern technology for you. Flawed.

Henry Yes. I suppose so. You won't mind lending me a couple of jugs full, will you? When I go. Georgina's probably dying for a cup of coffee.

Victor Please. Feel free.

Henry Thanks. (*He chuckles, suddenly*) Mind you, in a way I'm jolly glad they *hadn't* turned your water off.

Victor (*laughing*) Because you couldn't have had a cup of coffee!

Henry No, no! More important than that.

Victor More important than coffee? In what way?

Henry Well ... you obviously get quite emotional on the subject of public utilities.

Victor considers this for a moment

Victor Really? I didn't think I got awfully worked up about gas and electricity.

Henry And water?

Victor (*laughing*) And water!

Henry But you did.

Victor Sorry?

Henry You got *very* excited about water.

Victor Did I?

Henry Good Lord, yes! You even suggested that it was quite on the cards that we should come to fisticuffs because of it.

Victor Because of water?

Henry Yes.

Victor Ah... (*Realizing that this is to his advantage and becoming vehement on the matter*) Ah—well, yes! Yes, I—I *do* feel strongly! *Very* strongly! I can't stand inefficiently run utilities. It makes my blood boil!

Henry (*amused*) But not your water!

They laugh, then Henry becomes reflective

Sad, though, that a water crisis could bring out possible violence between neighbours...

Victor Well, that's human frailty for you.

Henry Yes. I suppose it is. Mind you— (*he laughs a little*) for a moment I thought that *you* thought that I was talking about something else.

Victor *Not* about water?

Henry No. Something more important than water.

Victor Nothing more important than water if coffee's at the top of your agenda! (*He laughs, then lets it die*) W-what sort of thing was that?

Henry Well ... you know ... the usual trouble.

Victor Oh? Which ... which usual trouble is that?

Henry You know! Women...

Victor Oh, *them*! Yes. Yes, they *can* be trouble, can't they?

Henry And that's what I thought *you* thought I was talking about!

Victor (*overdoing it a bit*) Did you really? Good Lord, no! Nothing like that!

Henry Not women, just water?

Victor Exactly!

They laugh together

Mrs Capstick pounds in from upstairs

Mrs Capstick You two going to sit down here all morning? I can't carry on in here if there are men sitting down.

Henry Mrs Capstick, you didn't find an ear-ring in here this morning, did you?

Mrs Capstick An ear-ring?

Henry Yes—you know— (*He mimes an ear-ring*)

Mrs Capstick I didn't know you went in for that sort of thing!

Henry It's not mine! It's my wife's.

Victor (*nervously*) *Your* wife's?

Henry Yes.

Victor Georgina's?

Henry Well, I haven't got any *other* wife!

Victor Why should one of Georgina's ear-rings be in here? Georgina wasn't here last night!

Henry No, no—Georgina wasn't wearing it at the time.

Mrs Capstick Then who *was* wearing it?

Henry *His* wife. (*He indicates Victor*)

Victor Rachel?

Henry Yes. She borrowed it last night.

Victor Borrowed an ear-ring?

Henry Well—two, actually. One on each ear. And she lost one. Not one ear, one ear-ring. She was looking for it in our house but she couldn't find it, so she thought she might have dropped it when she got home.

Mrs Capstick But why was your wife wearing another man's wife's ear-rings?

Henry Apparently the dress seemed to call out for them.

Victor What dress?

Henry The dress that Rachel was wearing last night. The one she borrowed from my wife.

Victor You mean she borrowed a dress *and* some ear-rings?

Henry Yes. And some shoes.

Victor But why was Rachel wearing somebody else's dress and ear-rings and shoes to look after an empty house?

Henry looks at him, blankly, for a moment

Henry Sorry?

Victor Mr Procter said that last night Rachel was house-sitting for you at number thirty-five!

Henry I wonder what gave him that idea…

Victor (*puzzled*) She was supposed to be rowing.

Mrs Capstick In a dress and ear-rings?

Henry Mrs Capstick, would you just get on with the cleaning?

Mrs Capstick I can't leave *this* conversation. It's far too interesting! (*She sits down with them, enthusiastically*)

Henry (*to Victor*) She *was* rowing.

Victor That's what I thought.

Henry Only she fell in.

Victor Fell in?!

Henry Yes. There was a storm. And she fell in.

Mrs Capstick *I* don't remember a storm last night.

Victor Neither do I…

Henry Well, she said it was more of a squall.

Mrs Capstick So she left the boathouse and went back to number thirty-five and borrowed your wife's dress and ear-rings?

Henry And shoes.

Victor (*suddenly realizing*) Good God! She might have come back here…!

Henry looks at Victor, thoughtfully

Henry You get awfully worked up about the strangest things, don't you? Water shortages and people falling in rivers.

Victor What I mean is—why did she go to *your* house?

Mrs Capstick She was soaking wet.

Henry Thank you, Mrs Capstick. (*To Victor*) She was soaking wet.

Victor (*quietly*) Lucky she didn't come straight home…!

Henry What?

Victor (*hastily covering*) Why didn't she come straight home? Then she needn't have borrowed somebody else's clothes!

Henry Apparently she hadn't got her key with her.

Victor But she had got *yours*?

Henry Yes. You remember. Georgina had given Rachel our spare key in case of an emergency.

Mrs Capstick Like falling in the river.

Henry What? Yes. Anyway, I'd better take some water home to Georgina so *she* can have some coffee.

Henry hastily finishes off his coffee and takes the empty cup into the kitchen

Mrs Capstick (*puzzled*) Take some water home? (*She looks inquiringly at Victor*)

Victor Never mind, Mrs Capstick. It's a long story.

Henry returns, smiling broadly, carrying the plastic bag containing Georgina's handbag

Henry Rachel's handbag turns up in the most unusual places…

Victor (*nervously*) What?!

Henry First of all it was in the wastepaper basket—now it's inside a plastic bag in the kitchen! (*He produces the handbag*)

Victor Ah! Yes…

Mrs Capstick That's not Mrs Parker's handbag! It's mine!

Henry Yours?

Mrs Capstick (*taking it, possessively*) Yes—definitely mine. Isn't it, sir? (*She grins at Victor, proud of her achievement*)

Victor Ah—yes—that's right…

Henry (*puzzled*) I thought you said—?

Victor I was confused.

Mrs Capstick Mr Capstick bought it for me last Christmas. (*She goes towards the front door*)

Victor (*rising, apprehensively*) *Now* where are you going?

Mrs Capstick Back to number thirty-five.

Victor What?!

Mrs Capstick I can't carry on here with men under my feet. (*She opens the door*)

Victor (*wildly*) You don't need to take your handbag with you! You can leave your handbag here—in the plastic bag—until you've finished!

Mrs Capstick I couldn't do that, sir. Somebody might pinch it.

Mrs Capstick winks and goes, leaving Victor in despair

Henry (*puzzled*) Everyone seems to have chosen the same handbag…
Victor Yes! I told you—they're very common! You can buy them anywhere. Hundreds of people have got them! I'll get you some water. (*He sets off towards the kitchen*)
Henry Yes—right! (*Following him*) And Victor——
Victor Yes?
Henry I can take Georgina's dress back at the same time.
Victor Oh—right…

Henry and Victor disappear into the kitchen as the Lights fade to Black-out

The Lights come up on Georgina's and Henry's house

Mrs Capstick marches in, still carrying the handbag, just as Georgina comes out of the kitchen with a mug of coffee

Georgina (*surprised*) Mrs Capstick! You should be at number ten.
Mrs Capstick There's been another change of plan. I'm doing you now and number ten at twelve.

Georgina glances nervously towards the kitchen

Georgina Well, it's not very convenient.
Mrs Capstick Nobody's considering *my* convenience. (*She puts the handbag down on the sofa table and heads for the bedrooms*)

Georgina sees the handbag and smiles, delightedly

Georgina Oh, good! You've found my handbag, Mrs Capstick! That *is* a relief, I can tell you.

Mrs Capstick hesitates, her mind making the obvious leap

Mrs Capstick *Yours?*
Georgina Yes.
Mrs Capstick You're … you're *sure* this is yours?
Georgina Of course I'm sure! (*Going to her, happily*) Where did you find it?
Mrs Capstick (*dithering*) Find it? I didn't find it! I was… Oh, my God! I— I can't stand here gossiping! You're paying me to work, not to talk about handbags! I'll carry on in the bedrooms.

Mrs Capstick darts out to the bedrooms

Georgina is left bewildered by her extraordinary behaviour

The front door opens and Henry comes in, carrying two jugs of water, followed by Victor

Henry Here we are! Help is at hand!
Georgina What on earth have you got there?

Henry holds up each jug in turn, smiling delightedly

Henry Water! Water!
Georgina (*having forgotten*) Why do we want water?
Henry Sorry?
Georgina Why are you carrying two jugs of water?
Victor Henry thought you'd be dying for a cup of coffee. (*He looks about, anxious as to the whereabouts of the handbag*)
Henry Yes. I've just had a cup with Victor. Nothing wrong with *his* water.

Victor sees the handbag on the sofa table and pounces on it

(*Noticing*) You've already *got* one. (*Turning to Victor*) Victor——

Victor is not paying attention

Victor!

Victor turns, nervously, hiding the handbag behind his back

Victor Sorry?
Henry Georgina's already got a cup of coffee.

Victor sees that Georgina has already got a cup of coffee

Victor Good Lord, so she has! (*Surreptiously, he opens the drawer in the sofa table*)
Henry (*to Georgina*) How did you manage that? I thought Rachel had used the last drop of water.

Victor drops the handbag into the drawer and pushes it shut, but not as quietly as he had wished

(*Reacting to the noise*) What was that?
Victor *I* didn't hear anything! (*He moves away, assuming an air of innocence*)
Henry I'll just put these in the kitchen. (*He goes towards the kitchen with the two jugs of water*)

Georgina No!
Henry What?

Georgina hastily intercepts him

Georgina You can't go in there!
Henry Why are you always trying to keep me out of the kitchen?
Georgina You can go in there later.
Henry But I want to go in there *now*! I can't stand about in the sitting-room holding two jugs or water.
Georgina But we don't want any water!
Henry Sorry?
Georgina We've got plenty of water.
Henry No, you haven't. The water's been turned off. You told me.
Georgina Well, now it's back on again!
Henry Is it?
Georgina Yes. They turned it back on again.
Henry Who did?
Georgina The people who turned it off! Ten minutes ago. So we don't need those jugs of water now.
Henry No, I suppose not. (*Turning to Victor*) Needn't have bothered, then, need we, Victor?
Victor (*dispiritedly*) No...
Georgina It was very kind of you, Victor, to offer to share your water with us, but now we don't need it. (*To Henry*) So you can take this water back to Victor's house.
Victor But I live at number ten.
Georgina Yes. I know.
Victor You can't expect Henry to carry two jugs of water all the way back to *my* house.
Georgina Well, he can empty them in the garden, then! After all this dry weather the plants will be glad of it.
Henry (*bewildered*) Why can't I empty them in the kitchen?

Rachel comes out of the kitchen and sees Henry with two jugs of water

Rachel Why are you carrying two jugs of water? Is the house on fire?
Henry We thought you'd be dying for coffee. So Victor kindly lent me some of *his* water.
Georgina (*over-doing it*) But now that the water's back on again, Henry wants to get rid of Victor's water—*in the kitchen*! Do you think that will be all right?

Henry and Victor exchange a look

Henry Why shouldn't it be all right? Anyway, it's not *Rachel*'s kitchen, it's *our* kitchen!

Rachel Of course it'll be all right, Henry.

Georgina (*anxiously*) Are you sure?

Rachel Yes—*quite* sure. (*Reassuringly*) It's a nice big—*empty*—kitchen, so there's plenty of room.

Victor He's only going to empty two jugs of water. He doesn't need much room for that!

Henry (*to Georgina*) Do I take it that I now have your blessing to empty these two jugs of water in the kitchen?

Georgina Yes, darling—of course.

Henry Thank you!

Henry raises his eyes to Victor and goes into the kitchen

Victor goes to Rachel, very concerned

Victor Darling, why didn't you *tell* me?

Rachel Tell you?

Victor I was bound to find out sooner or later. (*He puts an arm around her shoulders and leads her to the sofa, considerately*)

Rachel Er ... find out what?

Victor About you falling in the river.

Rachel (*relieved*) Oh, *that*...

Victor You never mentioned it last night.

They sit on the sofa

Rachel I ... I didn't want to worry you.

Victor You've never fallen in before.

Georgina Well, she's only been doing it for three weeks so she's bound to make mistakes. (*She grins at Rachel*)

Victor Lucky you'd given her your spare key, Georgina.

Georgina Yes, it was, wasn't it? (*She exchanges a look with Rachel*)

Victor What I can't understand is why Mr Procter thought you were house-sitting last night. Had he *seen* you here, then?

Rachel Ah—yes! He thought he'd heard burglars, and—being on Neighbourhood Watch—he came in to investigate.

Victor (*thinking hard*) And you told him you were house-sitting?

Rachel Well ... yes.

Victor Why didn't you tell him why you were really there?

Rachel Oh, I couldn't do that...!

Georgina (*quietly*) No, you certainly couldn't...!

Victor Why not?
Rachel It would have seemed so ... so feeble. Falling in the river! Mr Procter used to be in the SAS.
Victor Well, you could have told *me*—*I* wasn't in the SAS.

Mrs Capstick comes in from upstairs and sees them

Mrs Capstick Oh, you're all *here* now, are you? Plans have changed again and I've got to go back to number ten, is that it?
Georgina Of course not, Mrs Capstick. You finish off here.
Rachel (*smiling, playfully*) I've been hearing all about you, Mrs Capstick...
Mrs Capstick And I've been hearing all about *other* people!

Mrs Capstick darts a severe look at Georgina, which Georgina does not understand

Rachel How long have you been doing it?
Mrs Capstick (*blankly*) I beg your pardon?
Rachel Don't be shy. After all, you *have* won awards for it.
Mrs Capstick Awards for what?
Rachel Ballroom dancing!

Mrs Capstick stares at her, totally bewildered. Victor is frozen

Mrs Capstick Sorry?
Rachel I hear you're an expert ballroom dancer.
Mrs Capstick Oh, yes?
Rachel (*to Georgina*) Her tango was the talk of the town.
Georgina How exciting. (*To Mrs Capstick*) You never mentioned it.
Mrs Capstick No, I should think I didn't! (*To Rachel*) Who told you this?
Victor (*rising, nervously*) I'm afraid *I* did, Mrs Capstick.
Mrs Capstick *You?*
Victor Yes. I'm sorry. (*To Rachel, incensed*) I did ask you not to mention it to her, Rachel! I knew she'd be embarrassed. I'm sorry, Mrs Capstick. I knew I shouldn't have told anybody. I should have respected your privacy. But I was so excited about it that I simply had to tell someone. (*To Rachel*) I told you in the strictest confidence.
Mrs Capstick (*stunned*) I don't know what you're on about.
Victor Yes, you do! Of course you do! We talked about it this morning. You remember!
Mrs Capstick No, I don't!
Victor Yes, you do! I said that ballroom dancing was a wonderful thing to do, that you should be proud of it, that it was a—a *bonus* in your life.

Mrs Capstick Is *that* what you said?
Victor Yes.
Mrs Capstick A … a bonus?
Victor (*nodding, desperately*) Yes!

Whereupon, Mrs Capstick grabs Victor and they go into an elaborate tango. Georgina and Rachel watch in astonishment

Henry comes in from the kitchen and sees the amazing spectacle

Henry What the hell's going on?

Mrs Capstick and Victor stop dancing. Unseen by the others, he passes some money to her, which she conceals in the pocket of her apron. Victor sinks into the armchair, exhausted

Rachel Mrs Capstick was showing Victor a few steps.
Henry I wondered what she was doing!
Mrs Capstick Well, *now* perhaps I can carry on the kitchen? (*She starts to go, then remembers something*) Oh, by the way, Mrs Brent, I found your track-suit and put it in here out of the way. (*She takes Rachel's track-suit out of the box seat and hands it to Georgina*)

They all stare at the track-suit, Rachel rising, apprehensively

Henry (*puzzled*) Track-suit? (*He takes it from Georgina to get a closer look*) I didn't think you'd got a track-suit, darling.
Georgina (*quietly*) Neither did I…! (*She glances at Rachel*)
Mrs Capstick Took *me* by surprise, I can tell you. Funny place to hide a track-suit.
Henry Oh? Where *did* you find it, then?
Mrs Capstick (*pointing*) Under your sofa!

Mrs Capstick goes, laughing happily, into the kitchen

Henry looks, inquiringly, at Georgina

Henry I don't think I've ever seen you in a track-suit, darling.
Georgina Well, I… I don't wear one very often.
Henry (*laughing*) I didn't think you wore one at all! Have you taken up some sort of sporting activity on the quiet?
Georgina Well, you're out at the theatre every evening!
Henry So *that*'s when you do it? In the evening! (*He laughs*)

Victor has been staring at the track-suit and he now gets up and goes to get a closer look

Victor Wait a minute! Isn't this *your* track-suit, darling?
Rachel Well, they … they all look alike, don't they?
Victor Different colours.
Henry Yes. Some red and some blue.
Victor Even green, occasionally.
Henry Yes.
Rachel Well, it isn't mine!
Victor Yes, it is. I recognize it.
Henry Of course! You probably left it here last night after you fell in the river. (*Realizing*) So *that*'s what you were looking for?
Rachel Sorry?
Henry This morning! When I found you kneeling down in front of the sofa. I *thought* using a walking stick to find an ear-ring was a bit unlikely!
Victor I can't understand why you put your track-suit under Henry's sofa in the first place…
Rachel I—I didn't!
Henry Well, that's where Mrs Capstick says she found it.
Victor You weren't wearing a track-suit when you fell in the river, were you?
Rachel No—of course not!
Henry No. You were wearing that bright shirt and a pair of trousers, weren't you?
Victor (*surprised*) A shirt and trousers? To *row* in?
Georgina Will you both stop asking Rachel questions! You'll make her feel like a criminal.
Henry We're just interested, that's all.

An urgent knock on the front door. Henry goes to open it

Procter is there, his unseen dog pulling at the leash and barking

(*Glaring at him, belligerently*) You can't bring that dog in here!
Procter He'll wait outside.
Henry He certainly will!
Procter (*to his dog*) Sit. Sit! Good boy. Good boy…

Procter casts the leash aside and walks in, dragging Frank behind him

Henry Good heavens, it's the charity jogger! (*He closes the door on the dog and joins them*)
Procter For the second time this morning I've caught this person climbing over your garden wall.

Henry (*to Frank*) You've been here twice already?

Frank I'm afraid so…

Procter (*taking out his mobile*) I'd better contact Constable Weaver. He will wish to be apprised of the situation.

Rachel He only climbed over a garden wall.

Procter Twice!

Georgina There's nothing sinister about that. People often climb over garden walls when they're in a hurry.

Procter Only if the house is on fire. (*He taps away at his mobile*)

Victor (*laughing*) At least he's got some clothes on this morning, eh, Henry?

Henry (*laughing also*) Yes! And they fit him a damn sight better than they would have fitted Rachel!

Frank What are you talking about?

Henry (*indicating them*) These are the clothes that Rachel was wearing when she fell in the river. And instead of shrinking they seem to have stretched! (*He laughs, enjoying Rachel's discomfort*)

Georgina tries to urge Procter on his way

Georgina So there's nothing for you to worry about, Mr Procter. Please go and take your dog for a walk.

She pushes him towards the front door, but Procter resists

Procter Just a minute!

Georgina *Now* what?

Procter There's something I'd like to *see* before I leave…

Georgina And what's that?

Procter faces Frank with heavy suspicion

Procter I'd like to *see* some of the money that he's *supposed* to have been collecting for charity.

Frank remains silent

Well?!

Frank I… I haven't got any…

Procter Haven't *got* any? Then where is it?

Frank I… I wasn't collecting for charity!

Procter ponders, powerfully

Procter Well, if you weren't collecting for charity what were you doing here at number thirty-five last night, taking off your clothes, drinking wine and cooking "little bits" for a lady who lives at number ten?

A dreadful silence. Everybody realizes what Frank was doing, even Mr Procter, who is overcome with embarrassment, knowing that he has now put the cat very firmly among the pigeons

Ah-er-will you excuse me? I think my dog is in need of a walk.

Mr Procter dashes out of the front door, his dog barking enthusiastically

Victor is deep in thought

Victor Rachel...?
Rachel Y-yes, Victor?
Victor Does this sort of thing often happen when people go rowing and fall in the river?
Georgina I... I'm sure there's a simple explanation...
Rachel (*quietly*) I wish there *was*...!
Victor Henry! I think I need a whisky.
Henry Good idea. So do I.
Frank (*raising one arm, nervously*) Could ... could *I* have a whisky as well?

Henry looks at Victor, uncertainly. Victor nods agreement

Henry Right. (*He goes to pour three whiskies*)
Frank (*to Victor*) You're taking this very calmly.
Victor Well, it's not my whisky.
Frank No, I mean ... about...
Rachel (*outraged*) Yes! Why aren't you hitting him?
Victor Why should I?
Rachel Well, isn't that what men usually do in these circumstances?
Frank I don't want him to hit me!
Victor Of course you don't, Frank. We're far too civilised for that.
Henry Yes. Victor only gets emotional about public utilities. (*He arrives with three whiskies*) Whisky, Victor.
Victor (*taking it*) Thanks.
Henry Whisky, Frank.
Frank (*taking it*) Thanks.
Henry Whisky, Henry. Thanks.

They drink in unison. Rachel erupts, glaring at Victor

Rachel Well, I think you're absolutely disgraceful!

Victor (*puzzled*) Sorry? I think I've lost the plot. I thought it was *you* who was in the wrong.

Rachel Yes! I am. And *you* should be furious!

Victor I don't see why.

Rachel You're not even jealous!

Victor (*calmly*) Yes, I am.

Rachel Why don't you *hit* him, then?!

Frank Don't keep telling him to do that!

Victor I'm not *going* to hit him.

Rachel Why not?

Victor He's only just got his whisky.

Mrs Capstick comes in from the kitchen, carrying the two empty jugs

Mrs Capstick (*holding them aloft*) There's a strange pair of jugs in the kitchen.

Victor They're ours, Mrs Capstick. (*He puts down his glass and takes the jugs from her*)

Mrs Capstick Then they should be at number ten, not at number thirty-five!

Henry I borrowed them from Victor because of the water shortage.

Mrs Capstick I didn't know there'd been a water shortage. Bit early to be drinking, isn't it?

Henry (*calmly*) We're in the middle of a crisis.

Mrs Capstick I thought you might be!

Mrs Capstick goes back into the kitchen

Victor (*abruptly*) Right! Come on, Frank!

Frank (*nervously*) W-where are we going?

Victor To take these jugs back to my house. You can carry one, I'll carry the other.

Frank Oh … right. (*He puts down his glass and takes one of the jugs*)

Victor And you know what's going to happen *then*, don't you?

Frank looks at him in nervous apprehension

Frank No…

Victor smiles at him, happily

Victor We're going to have another large whisky! (*He starts to go*)

Frank follows him, bewildered

Frank I can't think why you're being so understanding about this...
Victor (*with a secret smile*) You'd never believe it if I told you!

Victor grins at Georgina and goes out with Frank

Mrs Capstick comes in from the kitchen. She is carrying the jacket Georgina brought back from the cleaners

Mrs Capstick I'll put this upstairs, shall I, sir?
Henry Sorry?
Mrs Capstick Your tweed jacket. Back from the cleaners.
Henry Oh, right. Thank you, Mrs Capstick.
Mrs Capstick Seems very peaceful in here. Do I take it the crisis is over? Didn't last long. If we have a crisis in *our* house it goes on for days! (*She starts to go*)
Georgina By the way, darling—the cleaners found a latchkey in one of those pockets.
Henry Really? *I*'ll take that, Mrs Capstick——
Georgina It doesn't seem to fit our front door, though.
Henry D-doesn't it?
Georgina No. I tried it.
Henry Good Lord... (*He starts to go*)
Georgina (*suspicion growing*) Henry...?
Henry (*stopping*) H'm?
Georgina There's something I don't understand.
Henry Really?
Georgina If that key doesn't fit *our* front door ... whose front door *does* it fit?

Henry grins, enigmatically

Henry Wouldn't you like to know...! (*He starts to go again*)
Georgina Henry!

He stops

  Where are you going?
Henry To have a dance with Mrs Capstick.

Henry scuttles out, taking the astonished Mrs Capstick with him

*Rachel and Georgina are left alone, each busy with her own thoughts...
Rachel sits on the sofa, dismally*

Rachel Well ... that's that, eh? I suppose Victor was bound to find out sooner or later.

Georgina Yes. I suppose so...

Rachel Somehow I don't think I'm really cut out for that sort of thing.

Georgina Rowing?

Rachel Men!

Georgina Oh.

Rachel Are *you*?

Georgina (*her mind elsewhere*) No. No, I suppose not. (*She looks about, trying to remember something*)

Rachel What are you looking for?

Georgina My evening bag. It was here just now. (*She looks in the drawer and finds it*) Ah! Here it is. (*She sits beside Rachel with her evening bag*)

Rachel sees it—and remembers it! She looks more closely

What's the matter?

Rachel Is *that* your handbag?

Georgina (*cheerfully*) Yes, of course. Why?

Rachel I've seen it before...

Georgina Well, I've had it a long time.

Rachel (*coldly*) I mean—*last night!*

Georgina W-what?

Rachel (*with dawning realization*) How the hell did *your* handbag get into the wastepaper basket in *our* house when you were supposed to be at the pictures?

Georgina I—I'm sure there's a good explanation...

Rachel (*realizing the truth*) Georgina...

Georgina gets up and makes a run for it

(*Following her, furiously*) Georgina!

Tango music floods in as Rachel pursues Georgina towards the front door

Henry and Mrs Capstick come in from upstairs and see them as they run out into the street. They look at each other in surprise

Henry
Mrs Capstick ⎫ (*together*) Ooooh!

They start to dance the tango

The Lights come up on Victor's and Rachel's house

Frank and Victor are coming out of the kitchen, each with a glass of whisky

Georgina runs in through the front door, hotly pursued by Rachel

Georgina runs between the men, who watch in surprise and raise their glasses to each other. Rachel runs over the sofa to cut off Georgina's escape. Georgina runs back between the men, pushing Frank on to the sofa as she does so. Victor shrugs and sits beside Frank, amused. Rachel chases Georgina to the front door, but Mr Procter appears in the doorway, driving them back inside. He comes in to survey the carnage as Georgina falls backwards on to the sofa between the men, and Rachel falls into Victor's lap, their legs pointing up in the air

At the same time, in the other house, Henry collapses on to his sofa with Mrs Capstick on top of him, one leg pointing skywards

And at that precise moment the music ends

Black-out

FURNITURE AND PROPERTY LIST

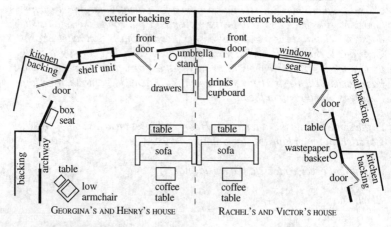

GEORGINA'S AND HENRY'S HOUSE   RACHEL'S AND VICTOR'S HOUSE

ACT I

On stage: **GEORGINA'S** AND **HENRY'S** HOUSE:
Sofa
Sofa table with drawer
Small armchair
Coffee table
Shelves and cupboard unit. *On it:* stereo, bottles of gin, whisky, tonic, glasses. *In it:* **Georgina**'s shirt and slacks
Chest of drawers. *In it:* plastic bag
Box seat
Umbrella stand. *In it:* 2 umbrellas, walking-stick
Carpet
Mirrors and pictures on walls

RACHEL'S AND **VICTOR'S** HOUSE:
Sofa. *On it:* **Victor**'s jacket
Coffee table
Drinks cupboard. *On it:* bottle of gin, whisky, tonics, lemon, 2 glasses, ice bucket
Wastepaper basket
Crescent table
Window seat. *On it:* tartan rug
Sofa table. *On it:* mobile phone

Wood flooring
Rugs

Off stage: Sports bag. *In it:* smart shoes, purse with 2 one pound coins (**Rachel**)
Plate of cocktail savouries (**Frank**)
Ice-bucket with 1/4 bottle of champagne, 2 champagne flutes (**Frank**)
Evening bag. *In it:* comb (**Georgina**)
Leash attached to unseen dog (**Procter**)
Open bottle of wine, 2 wine glasses (**Rachel**)
Towelling bathrobe (**Victor**)
Victor's suit (**Rachel**)
Frank's shirt and trousers (**Henry**)

Personal: **Frank**: **Georgina**'s apron
Victor: wristwatch, worn throughout
Procter: notebook, pen, mobile phone

ACT II

GEORGINA'S AND HENRY'S HOUSE:
Set: **Frank**'s trainers in drawer
Rachel's track-suit in box seat
Vacuum cleaner

RACHEL'S AND VICTOR'S HOUSE:
Re-set: Wastepaper basket

Set: Vacuum cleaner
Georgina's evening bag in drawer

Off stage: Mobile phone (**Henry**)
Dog leash (**Procter**)
Georgina's evening bag (**Mrs Capstick**)
Cup of coffee (**Rachel**)
Shopping bags—full, tweed jacket in cleaner's plastic bag (**Georgina**)
Mug of coffee (**Victor**)
Mug of coffee (**Henry**)
Tin of biscuits (**Victor**)
Mug of coffee (**Georgina**)
2 jugs of water (**Henry**)
2 empty water jugs (**Mrs Capstick**)
2 glasses of whisky (**Frank** and **Victor**)

Personal: **Victor**: 5 five pound notes
Procter: mobile phone

LIGHTING PLOT

Property fittings required: nil
Interior. Two living-rooms. The same throughout

ACT I   Summer evening

To open: Darkness

Cue 1   After house lights have faded   (Page 1)
         Bring up general lighting on Georgina's and Henry's house

Cue 2   **Frank** follows **Rachel** into the kitchen   (Page 6)
         Cross-fade to Rachel's and Victor's house

Cue 3   **Victor** and **Georgina** go into the kitchen   (Page 10)
         Cross-fade to Georgina's and Henry's house

Cue 4   **Rachel** goes into the kitchen   (Page 16)
         Cross-fade to Victor's and Rachel's house

Cue 5   **Victor**: "Where the hell has she got to?"   (Page 23)
         Cross-fade to Henry's and Georgina's house

Cue 6   **Henry** goes into the kitchen   (Page 31)
         Cross-fade to Victor's and Rachel's house

Cue 7   **Victor** moves towards the hall   (Page 34)
         Cross-fade to Henry's and Georgina's house

Cue 8   **Georgina** is going into the kitchen   (Page 37)
         Cross-fade to Victor's and Rachel's house

Cue 9   **Rachel** lifts **Georgina**'s evening bag   (Page 41)
         Bring up lights on Georgina's and Henry's house

Cue 10   **Rachel** and **Henry**: "Darling…?"   (Page 41)
         Black-out

Lighting Plot 87

ACT II   Summer morning

To open: Darkness

Cue 11	After house lights have faded *Bring up lights on Victor's and Rachel's house*	(Page 42)
Cue 12	**Victor** goes towards the bedrooms *Cross-fade to Henry's and Georgina's house*	(Page 48)
Cue 13	**Rachel** runs into the kitchen *Cross-fade to Victor's and Rachel's house*	(Page 51)
Cue 14	**Victor** goes into the kitchen *Cross-fade to Georgina's and Henry's house*	(Page 54)
Cue 15	**Rachel** and **Georgina** race out into the kitchen *Cross-fade to Victor's and Rachel's house*	(Page 60)
Cue 16	**Henry** goes into the kitchen *Cross-fade to Georgina's and Henry's house*	(Page 63)
Cue 17	**Georgina**, **Rachel** and **Frank** go towards the kitchen *Cross-fade to Victor's and Rachel's house*	(Page 66)
Cue 18	**Henry** and **Victor** go towards the kitchen *Cross-fade to Georgina's and Henry's house*	(Page 71)
Cue 19	**Henry** and **Mrs Capstick** start to dance *The Lights come up on Victor's and Rachel's house*	(Page 82)
Cue 20	**All** collapse on to sofas and music stops *Black-out*	(Page 83)

EFFECTS PLOT

ACT I